CAST

D0838980

CAST

THE TRUE STORY OF A MOM WHO LEARNED TO EMBRACE THE UNKNOWN THROUGH URBAN FISHING

Keep embracing your unknown!
Lisa Lax

LISA LILJEGREN

NEW DEGREE PRESS

COPYRIGHT © 2020 LISA LILJEGREN

All rights reserved.

CAST

The true story of a mom who learned to embrace the unknown through urban fishing

ISBN   978-1-64137-529-0   Paperback

          978-1-64137-530-6   Kindle Ebook

          978-1-64137-531-3   Ebook

My father, Mark Cody, is a legendary storyteller. Everything that happens around him and all the people he meets in his life become a little bigger, brighter, and funnier when he shares them using his inherent "Irish" filter. Through his eyes, the mundane becomes a story; the people he meets throughout his day become legendary by the time he gets home to tell about them.

All the events and people in this book are real, but the narrator has her father's Irish filter.

CONTENTS

—

"Mothers are all slightly insane."

—J. D. SALINGER, THE CATCHER IN THE RYE

PROLOGUE: A LICENSE TO CAST

———

It's amazing what twenty bucks will get you.

With just three quick clicks and a debit card, I became a licensed angler in the state of Wisconsin. Despite never having fished before, I purchased the credentials necessary to stand among the people who gathered nightly along the edge of the Milwaukee River. They didn't know who I was, but I'd watched them from afar. They intrigued me—I wondered about their lives and what brought them there together each night.

When I gathered up the courage, I reached out to a man I'd never met and asked him if he would introduce me to Milwaukee's urban fishing scene. After a brief text exchange about his father, he agreed to meet me in the epicenter of it all.

I first wound up on the banks of the Milwaukee River one night in late spring by accident. I had time to kill before picking up our son, Simon, from football practice. Kletzsch Park, the Milwaukee County park with the best access to the river, was a few blocks away from his gym. It was one of those hot flash spring evenings that gives hope that summer will indeed come. There were still pockets of snow on the ground, but I shed my coat anyway and welcomed the wet dewy air; it smelled of cold, fresh mud. It was dusk, not dark, and that, too, was promising. Since the riverbank was not visible from the road, I parked my car where I guessed the dam would be down below and walked toward an empty table hovering at the end of the bluff.

To my surprise, lined up along the bank and over the dam, a dozen men of all ages and races fished together, separately. In my brief time watching them that first night, they caught seven fish among them. I know the number because they marked their catches. There was a subtle choreography to the dance; they all seemed to know when one of them caught a fish. They stepped aside in unison to give the catcher some room, cocked their heads toward the scene, and nodded at the catch. The process was quiet, controlled, and mesmerizing.

I had to leave, but knew I'd be back.

* * *

As a wife and mother to a teenage son—about to leave home soon to go to college—I felt both pride and dread at the milestone our family was about to reach. We had become a "we of three" instead of a traditional family with two parents and a child. Our tiny, exclusive club was about to lose a founding member, and no change in our charter would stop this inevitability. Senior year in high school is a sustained paradox of firsts, lasts, and soons. Simon hadn't even had his first day of his last year in high school yet, and I was already feeling the loss.

We unintentionally built a social wall around our little family that kept us contently isolated from our adult peers and Simon's adolescent friends. At college, Simon would have to learn how to be young among young people. Brett and I would have to relearn how to be a couple with other couples. Perhaps most terrifying: I would have to learn how to be a woman without my sidekick of seventeen years.

All of this was heavy on my mind when I approached that riverside picnic table that first night.

A few months after Simon was born, we moved to a fine house with a big yard in one of the wealthiest suburbs in America. Our "fortress" is somewhat hard to find: on a dead-end street with no streetlights twenty miles from downtown Milwaukee. The time it takes to get from where we are now to our old apartment in the heart of Milwaukee, however, is decades past.

In the early 1990s, my husband and I lived in a historic, neoclassical apartment building on the corner of a twenty-four-hour intersection three blocks west of Lake Michigan. Brett moved to Milwaukee from Chicago after graduating with a creative writing degree from Columbia College, a liberal arts college located in the heart of The Loop. Since creative writing jobs were rather sparse, he worked as an assistant manager at a branch of The Gap near downtown. I was finishing up my senior year at Marquette University, a Jesuit university also in downtown Milwaukee, and worked in the security department at the nearby Milwaukee Public Museum.

Our neighborhood was young and conducive to going out. Armed with fresh degrees and surrounded by our best friends who settled within stumbling distance, we set out to transition from students to professionals. We lived on a bus line with a direct route to a strip of bars that featured nightly live music and quarter taps. Brett and I became local music groupies and crawled up and down the street to catch as many acts as we could, every night of the week. When bands weren't playing, their members were out supporting other bands. Our group of friends rotated among local band members who were on stage or in the crowd next to us.

Eventually, our friendships turned to business. At first, we simply worked the door at bars and collected the cover charge that went toward sound. Sound is the charge bands agree to pay up front to cover the sound equipment and the engineer to run it. There was no sliding scale for the bands: no matter the size of the crowd, the sound cost never changed. Each performance was, therefore, an investment with poor odds that already-broke bands made each time they got on stage. It wasn't long before we added our own investment into the experience. Some nights we lost our dinner money, others, we made enough to treat the band to an after-show early morning meal at the diner. Every night brought the thrill of being young, urban, and on the edge.

That was twenty-five years, seven jobs, three businesses, two moves, and a child ago. A child who, now, was about to go off to college. As the recruitment materials—with beautiful campus shots and headlines that read "Imagine yourself here," "Discover your potential," and "The most important decision of your life"—piled up on our kitchen counter, I realized that I, too, had important decisions to make. If I were the one receiving recruitment packages, they would read "What's ending?" or "What's next?"

* * *

I didn't know the circumstances of the fishermen I stalked but being a voyeur in their world reminded me of how Brett and I became known in Milwaukee music. We showed up nightly. Sat in the back. Appreciated their collective and individual skills. We spoke up when we were confident and fluent in their world. And we invested in the experience.

After hanging out on the picnic table over the dam for a couple of weeks, I was ready to take my fishing fangirl status to the next level. I had been showing up nightly to appreciate their catches. To become fluent, I would have to invest in the experience.

Anyone over the age of sixteen needs a license to catch a fish in Wisconsin. This is true for residents and out-of-state anglers alike. As a resident and first-time applicant, I opted for the most basic license at a cost of twenty dollars. They can be purchased online at the Wisconsin DNR website or at multiple retail stores that have an outdoor department. Most of the people I met along the way considered Walmart to be their annual fishing headquarters. The penalty for fishing without a valid Wisconsin fishing license starts at a hundred dollars.

I had never fished before. I didn't like to eat fish. And I've always been a card-carrying member of the squeamish club whenever I came into contact with anything smelly, slimy, or squirmy. Yet, there was something about the act of fishing and the people who were doing it that compelled me to come back to the river again, and again, and again.

Henry David Thoreau once wrote, "Many men go fishing all of their lives without knowing that it is not fish they are after."

Thoreau is one of America's most famous writers and is best known for *Walden*, a masterpiece written while living closely with nature on Walden Pond. In 1845, Thoreau confined himself to a remote cabin, owned by his friend and fellow writer Ralph Waldo Emerson. For two years, he lived, wrote, and thought almost completely in commune with nature. His work would inspire a generation of writers, environmentalists, and naturalists, which earned him the nickname of the "Father of Environmentalism." I remembered reading some of Thoreau's work when I worked as a marketing and special events coordinator within the Milwaukee County Parks System. He had so many good lines about man and nature that I often turned to him to help me write compelling copy.

I recalled his fishing quote nearly verbatim one evening as I watched the men of different ages, colors, and sizes stand together at the river instead of at their homes with their families. I wondered if they knew what they were after. Then I realized that I was also there instead of at home with my family. What was it that I was after? What answers could the river offer me?

I was a middle-aged mom on the verge of change, feeling trapped in my daily routine and helpless to the inevitable shifts life was throwing at me. My mindset going into my son's senior year of high school was that everything would be over soon. I anticipated a new quiet rhythm of binge television, early dinners, and Sunday drives when he left home.

We'd had a good run. I had an exciting life. It was time to wind down.

I knew I wasn't after fish even before I purchased my license. What I was hoping to find through the process was simply my "next." I was looking to meet new friends, try interesting experiences, and discover new passions that would fill my time and bring me back to the city of

Milwaukee. It was my constant quest for "next" that would lead me on a journey to my "after."

After becoming a licensed fisherman, I made new friends, like Angel who gave up his precious Sunday mornings to spend with me in the canals in the middle of the city. And Keith, who allowed me to tag along with him as he hosted a big family tournament and shared stories about his beloved father. Geoff, who met me between headlining gigs at Summerfest during his swing through Milwaukee. Dana, who trusted me with her story. And countless others who saved a spot for me along the river.

CHAPTER ONE

MY STORY

With both cheeks planted squarely on the base of the Golden Gate Bridge, I completed my sophomoric goal of bi-coastal monument rumping (otherwise known as sitting on the base of a state monument). It was for the sheer buffoonery of it all. That triumph in 1999 capped off a rear-ending world tour that started with the Brooklyn Bridge and went on to include the Eiffel Tower, the Louvre, the Bellagio Hotel and Casino in Vegas, the Sear's Tower in Chicago, and Pike's Fish Market in Seattle.

The hardest part of putting a butt on a monument is getting close enough to do so undetected. Not that it's necessarily illegal to plant a fully clothed cheek on a public monument, but it's weird enough to be called in for questioning. And it's difficult to have a sober reply when caught.

This silly tour started in New York with my husband Brett's family when we traveled to the East Coast to attend a wedding. The rehearsal dinner for the event was at a Michelin Star-rated restaurant at the base of the Brooklyn Bridge. We felt rather "Midwestern" at the fancy affair; me in my long flowing skirt and Brett in his khakis and a jacket—we missed the suggested attire mark by a couple of diamonds and cufflinks. Brett, his younger brother Wade, and I stepped outside to get some air and admire the view of the water and the bridge above. For no good reason, I walked directly to the bridge and rubbed my flowy-skirted butt on the base. It made the three of us laugh because with that spontaneous move we confirmed what was clearly evident: we were country fish in big city water.

Ann, my older sister by two years, lived in San Francisco that year for a job that frequently dispatched her to different parts of the world. She worked for a Palo Alto-based company in the tech industry and was in a circle of friends who had become overnight millionaires at the dawn of the dot-com boom. She is bilingual in Spanish and English and can communicate passably in Japanese, French, and Portuguese. As a student at the University of Minnesota, she earned her master's degree in International Human Resources and was the president of an organization that connected college students for business purposes from around the world. Always up for an adventure, she hosted me for a weekend to help me pull off my *coup de grâce*. Her unique paradox of sophistication and silliness made her my perfect accomplice.

On the first day of my visit, we stormed Napa Valley. We started our tour at the V. Sattui Winery in Saint Helena where the two of us split a bottle of Cab and enjoyed a fine snack tray of artisanal cheeses. Our next stop was the Frog's Leap Winery where we took the farm tour of the vineyards and enjoyed generous pours of Sauvignon Blanc and a loaf of crumby bread. On our way back through Napa, we stopped at Monticello Vineyards for a quick, crisp Rosé before hitting our final stop: the Jelly Belly Candy Company in Fairfield. We hopped on a guided tour and gorged ourselves on free popcorn-flavored jelly bellies until the sugar rush karate chopped any lingering wine buzz between us. When we finally left the candy company, we were sober and had sour stomachs that stuck with us all the way back to Palo Alto.

The second day we spent in San Francisco hitting all the postcard sites from Lombard Street to the Haight-Ashbury District to China Town. We also drove the famous streets featured in my favorite movie of all time: *Foul Play*, starring Chevy Chase and Goldie Hawn. Though billed as a comedy the 1970s film was more of a thriller, inspired by Alfred Hitchcock films. The movie—with classic villainous archetypes including a "dwarf" and an "albino"—was a great caper that involved an implausible plot to kill the Pope, and a romance between a cop and his damsel in distress. All of the scenes were shot beautifully throughout San Francisco. Like Graceland to Elvis fans, this was my Mecca.

My final day we had previously plotted for weeks. Our plan was for my butt to make contact with the base of the Golden Gate Bridge. That way my tour, which had started at an iconic New York bridge, would end in California at another iconic bridge.

On the morning of our big escapade, we parked inconspicuously a couple hundred feet away from the bridge at a spot Ann had already staked out. We hoofed our way around a barricade and through a grassy, bee-filled field in need of mowing. I packed good tennis shoes for this very trek but was remiss in planning for field op coverage for my legs. Without questioning my sanity, Ann was not only along for the ride but was a co-conspirator and chief schemer in my rump plan—just because it sounded fun.

This was at a time when our nation was more relaxed about barricades around monuments and structures. I imagine two yahoos attempting such an adolescent prank would be more scrutinized in today's environment.

We executed our plan, put our behinds on the bridge, and left laughing hysterically in a matter of twenty minutes. Our story about the adventure easily lasted twice as long.

* * *

I come from a family that appreciates a great story and an excellent adventure. My dad, Mark Cody, is Irish: loves his beer, loves his girl (my mom), and has a booming voice that could put Vincent Price to shame. He uses those traits to tell exquisitely epic tales of our ancestors that may or may not be true. Regardless, because they've been told so often, they are a proud part of our heritage. Almost all of his stories begin the same way, "It's really kinda funny," he starts out of nowhere. This phrase then turns into a story, one that is usually not funny at all. Quite often people actually die in the stories he begins this way. When our whole family is participating in a conversation and my dad interjects with his "It's really kinda funny," Brett is the first to chime in, "Oh no, who dies?" That interruption never deters my father from finishing his story. Nothing does.

My mom, Mary Ann Halbach Cody, is a hardworking German farm girl. Her mom, sisters, brother, and all of the descendants who grew out of their Wisconsin farm, have a different way of viewing the world. They survived off the land and had to battle the Midwest's mercurial climate to take care of the animals, manage crops, and plan for harvest. They eked out a living and created a life legacy of hard work, family first, and an all-in community focus that has shaped and molded the entire next generation. They taught us to work together, cackle when we laugh, love family with mama bear ferocity, and serve the right snack for every occasion. For people who carried the weight of the world on their shoulders, they always made time for cold beer, Kielbasa, the Green Bay Packers, and Sheepshead whenever we stopped by—which was often.

Sheepshead is a complicated card game from Germany that involves tricks, trumps, blinds, and schmears. It takes a lifetime to learn, and the masters of the game were my aunts, uncles, and cousins who lived in the farming communities throughout Southeastern Wisconsin.

My mom and her immediate family left the farm when she was a junior in high school and moved to the mid-sized Wisconsin town where I was eventually raised. She finished school and put herself through college, where she studied to be a teacher by working late shifts at a twenty-four-hour diner in the town's bar district. My father, being Irish and imbibing of his beloved beer, frequented the diner at bar time and fell in love with the no-nonsense coffee waitress from a farm.

On my dad's eightieth birthday, just shy of their fifty-first wedding anniversary, I tweeted a self-penned limerick to my Twitter account that summed up all that is important to the two of them:

"*To young Mark there was no one finer,*
than the waitress he met at Webb's diner.
They had three babies, who became adoring ladies,
Together, let's all raise a steiner."

The third "adoring lady" is my younger sister by nine years, Paula. She is brilliant. She earned her medical degree from the Medical College of Wisconsin and heads up an adolescent medicine clinic in Madison. She has since earned a master's degree in public health. Nothing phases her. She can dance, write, cook, sew, shop, decorate, and drink like your best girlfriend. At the same time, she is a nationally respected doctor who will stay up with you all night when your kid is sick. Her mind is so open and non-judgmental that teenagers easily ask her their most personal and embarrassing questions about sex, eating disorders, body dysmorphia, and abuse and get from her satisfying, empowering answers.

Paula was just seven years old when I got sick. I was about to enter senior year in high school and could barely leave the house because of stomach pain and digestion insecurities. Even at her young age, Paula was a natural caretaker and medical scientist. She paid attention to things like cause and effect and carefully tracked what I ate and how my body responded to it down the road. When we finally got my diagnosis of Crohn's Disease nearly two years after suffering the first symptoms, Paula helped me manage my new medications, restricted diet, and pain so I could finish school and feel confident going on to college.

It was no surprise to anyone that she would become a doctor. I've been in and out of remission several times since my teenage diagnosis, with symptoms getting progressively worse with each return. Paula was and remains my greatest advocate and fiercest protector.

We sisters gathered for a girls' weekend at Newport Beach in Rhode Island for a summer getaway before Paula entered medical school. We had an important mission that required the three of us to put together our best minds. Our father was about to retire from his long career as a social worker within the Wisconsin prison system and we needed to present him with an appropriate gift. Having drained all our funds on our fabulous weekend, we decided the best course would be to develop a retirement scavenger hunt with a glorious prize for him at the end—should he accomplish his mission. This obviously allowed us time to kick the gift can down the road.

Over four bottles of wine and aged cheddar cheese from Vermont, we created the most elaborate, impossible-to-accomplish scavenger hunt our over-served sister minds could conjure up. We had my parents placing big bets in Vegas, visiting remote inns throughout the Midwest, trying elaborate foods, and buying hard-to-get tickets to inconvenient events. To our surprise, our parents accomplished each and every item on the list within one year and took the pictures to prove it. Their glorious prize turned out to be them treating us and our husbands to a wonderful, multi-course dinner at a restaurant in Milwaukee. I'm not sure they thought the prize was worthy of their herculean effort, but we were sure pleased with our gift.

After living around the world, Ann is now a language teacher in Cape Cod, Massachusetts. She and her husband, Michael, who is trilingual in English, Spanish, and German and owns a large real estate company, have two teenage boys, Alex and Charlie. Through this, they manage to maintain a robust international lifestyle with friends and family from all over the world.

Paula and her husband, Matt, live in Madison, Wisconsin. She heads her adolescent medial practice, and Matt is a civil engineer who works on some of the largest highway projects in the state. They have a daughter who is already showing promising signs of carrying on the Cody sister traditions. She is named Cecilia Rose after our grandma, the matriarch on our farmer side.

Grandma Cecilia watched Paula every day after school, so the two of them were extra close. Grandma didn't drive, which meant that their daily activities were limited to what the two of them could come up with in the backyard. They danced, chased butterflies, worked in the garden, and watered plants. These, of course, sound like traditional activities, but our grandma was anything but traditional. She was tough talking, loud swearing, hardworking, and mad laughing.

When I was little I heard stories about a western lady named Calamity Jane and was convinced that she was actually my grandmother. It became a tradition in our family to play the song "Cecilia" by Simon & Garfunkel at weddings and do a cousin conga line around the dance floor and throughout the venue in her honor. When my grandma got older she'd lead the parade in her wheelchair, pushed by one of her many grandchildren. At her funeral, Paula brought a boom box so we could dance one more time together to her song. She pressed play and held the big box up dramatically over her head like the guy in *Say Anything*. She bounced back and forth in place to the familiar beat to give everyone a chance to finish up their ham and turkey bites before joining her in a final conga line.

Only nobody got up.

They stared at Paula, slightly paralyzed at the prospect of dancing at a person's funeral; even the funeral of a person as fun-loving and rule-breaking as our grandma. When it became apparent that no one else was getting up, I put down my own fork and danced my way up to her. We bounced and bobbed awkwardly to the song while the rest of our family stayed seated and smiled knowingly at our clumsy tribute. It turns out the song drags on a bit toward the end.

We all talk with each other daily in a family group text that has existed for several years. Simon started the thread as a way to debate sports, specifically the rivalry between the Patriots and the Packers. Ann's East Coast in-laws were as proud of their Patriots as we were of our Green Bay Packers. For a family of girls, we were raised to be avid sports fans and took all our home teams, especially the Green Bay Packers and the Milwaukee Brewers, very seriously. Of course, it helps that both my sisters married men who are also sports fans. I am proud and lucky to call them my brothers.

I'm convinced that Simon was born obsessed with sports. As soon as he could talk he rattled off athletes and their numbers. By the time he turned ten, he had analyzed current and historical stats for fun and watched any and all programs he could about athletes and the challenges they overcame to become champions. He put all this knowledge into good use by appointing himself commissioner of several online family sports leagues. Now, if there's a line on something sports-related in Vegas, we're making our picks in the family text.

* * *

These are the people I confided in when I decided I wanted to learn to urban fish. I described to them what I had witnessed along the banks of the river. I explained that I'd been killing time creeping the dam and how captivated I became with the idea of going out there and giving it a try. I thought I sounded pretty convincing.

"But, you don't like fish," noted Paula with a high degree of skepticism. "What would you do if you actually caught one?"

"Throw it back," I responded as if I didn't understand the larger meaning of her question.

She was right. I hated fish. I had no idea what I would do when I caught one. The guys on the river were so smooth with their releases, they made it look easy. I figured I'd know what to do when the time came. But she didn't actually care about that; she's used to asking questions to get people talking. What she really wanted to know, and what I couldn't yet answer, was "Why fishing?"

I hadn't yet articulated my anxiety to my family about Simon going away to school, though the sense of change coming was palpable to all of us. The idea that our kids—our sons, daughters, nieces, and nephews—would move on and create lives of their own was an abstract one for all of us. Until now. We were all losing our collective firstborn. It wouldn't just be the big stuff like Christmas morning that would change, it's all the little stuff too: daily sports updates, car rides, practice schedules, and homework. All that would stop, all at once.

At first, I wasn't looking to redefine myself. I just needed something to do. And, I needed new people in my life to do things with. I found urban fishing by accident. I described to my sisters the serene scene along the river and the quiet subtleties of the people who demonstrated a patience that I didn't possess. I told them that I channeled wisdom in the rolling water and shady trees. When I sat on the picnic table in the sun, watching strangers cast like artists, I explained to them that I felt the kind of small that mothers don't ever allow themselves to feel: powerless and out of control.

I could not force my family's future. I couldn't stop time. And I couldn't make this year of lasts less monumental. So, I thought I would fish. It didn't make a lot of sense, but then again nothing did.

After my very first outing, I thought about my family's traditions. Maybe my adventure would lead to the next great story. "It's really kinda funny..."

CHAPTER TWO

LISTEN FOR THE BELLS

—

It's true what they say about goldfish: they grow to the size of their bowl. This was evident at a recent family fishing tournament hosted in a Milwaukee County park by a family that has been synonymous with Milwaukee urban fishing for nearly fifty years. A goldfish was the largest catch of the day and the proud, young angler took home the hundred-dollar prize. It wasn't your standard kids' bedroom goldfish, however. This prize fish adapted to its large lagoon home and measured in at just under nine inches.

The young man who reeled in the prize-winning catch was so excited he fell into the lagoon.

According to Keith—the organizer of the event and son of a Milwaukee urban fishing legend—in the twenty-four years that his family hosted fishing events, no one has ever fallen in the water. It was a day of firsts because, in the history of the fishing tournament, no goldfish has ever garnered the top prize.

"Goldfish aren't supposed to be in here, they aren't stocked by the Department of Natural Resources, but we see them once in a while. They were likely someone's pet first," surmised Keith. While Goldfish aren't stocked in Wisconsin waters, several other fish are—trout, salmon, bass, sturgeon, and pike are among the DNR's long list.

Keith and the dozen or so dads handled the kid-overboard like pros. The boy was swiftly pulled out of the water, and the men focused on the gold, glistening prize-winning fish instead of the sheepish, dripping young man holding it. Confidence, self-esteem, fatherhood, self-reliance…there is a lot packed into urban fishing events like these. Keith's father understood what the simple act of fishing could do for one's soul, one's family, and one's community. He spent a large portion of his life making an impact on Milwaukee from every little beginner's angle.

I met up with Keith at a scheduled free fishing event at a Milwaukee park, situated in the heart of the city with a large lagoon. The event was packed with young, smiling anglers and their parents. Many were trying fishing for the very first time. As Keith took it all in, he shook his head and said to me, "My dad would have loved this right here."

His father spent his career as a park worker for Milwaukee County. When he wasn't servicing the grounds, he was inspiring kids. He kept his truck full of rods and bait and during his off hours, he introduced young ones who frequented the parks to his great joy in life. In the mid-nineties, he started a bi-weekly fishing club so that kids knew exactly where and when they could find their patron saint of urban fishing.

While his fishing club no longer meets, the annual tournaments remain anticipated events in the community and a family tradition his son, Keith, is proud to carry on.

"Fishing is a thing that I enjoy doing because it was my bonding time with my brother and dad," said Keith. "When we went fishing it was us three against the world…or us three against the fish," he joked with a deep, infectious laugh.

Keith is on a mission to continue his father's fishing legacy. "If I get an opportunity to help a kid fish, my whole day is fulfilled."

When he's on his own time, Keith prefers catfishing—especially with his brother, who is partial to fishing for crappie. They have to find water spots that offer both.

"My brother would pick me up at four in the morning and the two of us would be out there with our cigars in peace for hours," he said. "You can catch catfish in almost every Wisconsin river. Except you won't find any here at this park unless somebody dumped some in."

If you've never seen a catfish, you should know that they are horrible to look at. They have long whiskers, big heads, and cylindrical bodies. They don't have scales, either. Some species of catfish make breathing possible by coating their own naked skin with mucous—so they're slimy. Others have bony plates that serve as body armor. Crappies are popular "pan fish," which means they are good to eat and generally don't grow much larger than the size of a frying pan. They're also easier on the eyes than catfish. They are in the sunfish family and closely resemble a classic kid's drawing of a fish.

Years ago, along with their father, the men erected a bell system to their pulls so they would know when a fish tugged on their lines in the dark. They choose to fish within hearing distance to the bells, so they can help each other reel fish in. Keith and his brother enjoy the idea of fishing alone, together, and prefer to fish overnight at a dark, secluded spot. They fish apart but stay in bell distance of one another.

"We stay close by, listening for the bells," said Keith.

Their dad no longer fishes. He almost died doing what he loves a few years ago.

"My dad went fishing like he always did and got a hook stuck in his hand," Keith explained.

According to Keith, his dad is terrified of needles and didn't go in for a check-up and a tetanus shot after the incident. He chose to keep the injury to himself. It was on a Mother's Day when he was getting ready to head out to the water and landed in the emergency room with a near catastrophic infection instead.

"We almost lost him because he didn't do what he knew he needed to do," says Keith. "My dad retired in the hospital because he didn't want a little needle."

Keith didn't always enjoy fishing with his dad. He stepped away from it entirely for a little more than a decade when he was a young adult. Now, as a father of four adults and a grandfather to five, Keith hopes that his own children will follow a similar path of making their way back to their father through fishing. He taught all his kids to fish when they were young.

"My oldest is thirty-two years old, around the age that I was when I came back to fishing with my dad," said Keith. "I'll keep a pole ready for all of them whenever they want to join me again." He estimates that he keeps over a hundred poles in his garage ready, so that shouldn't be a problem.

It wasn't just fathers and sons at the fishing tournament. Moms fish, too.

I met a mom named Rhonda, her husband, and their youngest son, Cameron, at the urban fishing tournament. Rhonda has fished nearly her entire life. Like so many kids, she learned from her father. She grew up about ninety minutes northwest of Milwaukee along the great Fox River and returns there to fish with her family when she can.

Like Keith, she's drawn to catfish. The look of the fish has never bothered her. Rhonda is a self-described "expert fish cleaner" and has been cleaning fish since she was a little girl. She recalls that her father would come home from a day of fishing with a full bucket of fish and be so proud of his catch that it made her feel good to clean them. It still does.

During our conversation I mentioned Thoreau's quote, "Many men go fishing all of their lives without knowing that it is not fish they are after," to her and asked what she thought that meant.

"To me, fishing was always about being with my dad," said Rhonda. "It was such a part of my life that it's important for me to carry on this tradition with my own kids." She paused for a second and then added, "but it was also about the fish."

Rhonda is made tough. So tough that she even fishes with homemade stink bait on occasion. The worst part, she mentions, is having to ride with the heinous concoction in the car. Stink bait is like grandma's apple pie in some fishing families. The recipes are not written down; they are passed on from generation to generation. Unlike grandma's kitchen, this important ritual takes place in garages and backyards across the state. Secret ingredients and proprietary stink-bolstering methods are whispered in hushed reverence from lips kissed with Miller High Life, the champagne of beers.

Most of the recipes listed online include liver and time in the heat. Almost all add a special warning to avoid preparing indoors. Beyond those staples, the ingredients vary. Some call for sardines and sardine oil. Other revealed ingredients are moldy cheese, beef blood, garlic, and flavored Jell-O.

Twenty years ago, I accidentally came across a bucket of stink bait while walking through the garden park where I worked as a marketing and events director. I had just graduated from college and accepted this highly coveted position at the Mitchell Park Horticultural Conservatory. The Conservatory is often referred to as "the Domes" by locals, for the three conoidal garden domes that provide a curvaceous element to Milwaukee's skyline.

Each dome is 140 feet in diameter and built with a cast-concrete undercarriage covered by a steel-and-glass shell. Each of the three domes represents a distinct horticultural region of the world: the Floral Dome for seasonal and holiday shows, the Arid Dome featuring plants from Africa and Americas, and the Tropical Dome housing thousands of species of plants. A central lobby connects the three domes.

The park surrounding our Domes had a lagoon that was a popular fishing hole for nearby residents. Over lunchtime one day I strolled around the lagoon and was accosted by a smell so heinous I swear it made my nose bleed. I saw a few of the guys in overalls standing around a bucket who were clearly noseblind to the apocalyptic stench thickening the air and clogging my pores.

Hesitating to get any closer, I shouted, "What is that awful smell?!" They seemed rather proud of themselves that their stink bait recipe had reached my nostrils up on the walkway. So proud, in fact, that they revealed their carefully guarded secret ingredient—fried chicken.

Rhonda is chatty and shares stories about how she got each one of her children fishing young. They all learned while wearing life vests, which is a good thing because when a fish hits, the tug can be startling. Her one rule for all of her young children? "If dad or me aren't here to help you, don't try to reel it in by yourself. Drop the pole and run."

* * *

As soon as I discovered the secret world of urban fishing, I was eager to visit more city spots where I'd heard that the fish bite. One evening I drove to a park on the Milwaukee River that had been known to be family-friendly. Up above the riverbank were some playground equipment and a dog walking area. I'm told that down below, hidden from the crowds, was a site frequented by serious fishermen.

It was still cold, and though the snow had melted, the wet draft of spring was too uncomfortable to be out in for any length of time. It was dusk. The path to get down to the infamous spot was slick, and I needed both hands to stabilize myself on the uneven stones. I arrived at a footbridge just above a dam and kept walking, gingerly, along the firm mud path. There wasn't anyone out that night; still I kept walking.

As I approached a masterful graffiti wall, I crossed paths with an African American man about my age. This was at a blind point in the path where both directions were camouflaged by branches. Neither of us expected to run into anyone. We greeted each other rather abruptly and kept moving our separate ways. When we had gained about fifteen feet of distance between us, I heard his baritone voice behind me, "Ahh, miss, you probably shouldn't go any farther."

I turned around and faced the man who had also stopped to face me. We stared at each other for a second. Then I simply said, "Thank you," and reversed my steps to walk toward him. He didn't wait for me and also kept walking. I don't know what was at the end of the path but was glad to be led out by this man who watched out for a stranger.

A few months later, at that very same park, it was discovered that a man was living in an underground bunker with a mess of weapons and ammunition, just steps from the river's edge. Despite my many river visits, I don't recognize his picture that is now plastered everywhere but am reminded, once again, to be smart. A former football player friend once told me that he won't go urban fishing anywhere near Milwaukee without his gun (he is licensed to carry a firearm). When I pressed him to explain what he was worried about, he admitted he'd never seen anything that made him feel uneasy; he simply was afraid of the unknown at the water's edge.

The Milwaukee River divides the city into East and West sides. It starts in the county where I was born and rolls about a hundred miles south, where it joins two other major rivers— the Menomonee and Kinnickinnic—in the heart of Milwaukee, before flowing into Lake Michigan. The three rivers were first home to many Native American tribes and served their vital needs for thousands of years. European explorers recognized the area's abundance of water and decided the Great Lakes location would be a major asset to their industrious objectives. They then, of course, employed brutal, dishonest tactics to displace the Native Americans.

Business boomed in the nineteenth and twentieth centuries thanks to Milwaukee's abundant water supply. First it was the brewing industry, then tanning, brick, wheat, and meat-packing followed. Not only did these industries need ample freshwater, they also relied on the transportation and shipping grid that the flowing waters provided. But prosperity came with gross and toxic consequences. The rivers had been the dumping ground for business and human waste.

Throughout most of the twentieth century Milwaukeeans did what they could to avoid the smelly, discolored, debris-filled waterways. Everything in Milwaukee waters or near them was considered contaminated—especially the fish.

Since the late 1980s, significant efforts have been put into place to reclaim the waters, revitalize the riverfronts, and restore the ecosystem. The rivers are now a main attraction in the city of Milwaukee. Bars and restaurants have cropped up along a river walk, canoes and kayaks litter the rivers on a typical Saturday afternoon, and high-end condos line the water's edge. People like what is offered on the surface but are still understandably skeptical about what lies below. Very few people urban fish in Milwaukee, and even less eat what they catch.

* * *

When Keith agreed to meet me at the Milwaukee River for my first lesson, I looked at it as a social occasion that warranted snacks. We made arrangements by text. After getting the specifics out of the way—license, time, location—I wanted to get down to the important business. What could I bring to eat? I offered to pick up dinner and texted a few options. No response. I thought maybe he wasn't looking to spend that much time with me, so I, instead, offered to pick up some beers and chips. Again, no response.

It was getting close to the time that I was to leave work to meet Keith at the river and he finally texted three words: "Water is fine." So, I ran to the store and picked up four different flavored waters, chips, and gummy worms because every meeting must include some form of sustenance. As it turned out, he didn't have his own fishing license yet. He hadn't made the annual trip to Walmart to renew for another season. As my instructor, he was limited in what he could teach me. I took out my phone and showed him where he could do it online in just a few clicks and he agreed to look into it. I'm sure he stuck with his Walmart ritual because, as I would learn throughout the summer, the trip to Walmart is a sacred day for fishermen: it's the day they proclaim their new season to open.

Keith isn't chatty when he fishes. I came in hot with a lot of questions about bobbers, lures, and rods. When I noticed that our conversation was mostly one-sided, I apologized to him for talking so much. He stopped, looked me in the eyes, and said, "There is never a dumb question. You're trying to learn something entirely new. If we knew everything we wouldn't have to depend on other people."

He taught me to cast without a hook. I side-armed back and forth a couple of times and—even without a hook—got my line wrapped around a low-hanging branch. He stepped out far closer to the edge than I would have to rescue it. I sheepishly apologized for such a silly mistake. He responded reassuringly, "When you just start off you have to keep developing your craft. Everybody makes it look easy, and it's not. I can promise you that."

Despite my barrage of questions, he remained kind, patient, and guarded about his personal life. He told me that one family story about their fishing bells, and then he owned his silence. I finally followed his lead and concentrated on my body movements, taking in the scenery silently for the rest of our time together. It might not have been soon enough, however, because Keith stopped answering my texts when I inquired about a second lesson. That one outing would be our only.

I learned a lot from Keith, that first day. Most notably, how to behave as a fisherman. I learned that I didn't have to fill silences with chatter and snacks. Instead, I should practice being quiet and still, like Thoreau when he immersed himself in the Walden woods.

I learned to pay attention to the beauty around me and appreciate this time and place as a respite of the week; instead of invading this sacred space with meaningless chatter, just taking a moment to listen for the bells.

CHAPTER THREE

SLEEP WELL AND DREAM BIG

——

Hidden deep in the junk section of my red wallet was a doubled-up, yellow Post-it note with careful, hand-drawn lines, pressed down firmly and measurably by tiny hands. In between the lines were words written in penmanship often praised by elementary teachers and worthy of re-posting on the family refrigerator. The words:

> "man, he thought.
> He had come to the
> town only to find
> a woman who could
> interpret his dream.
> The Alchemist
> 17%"

I didn't remember how this got there and couldn't quite place the writing or the context. I've carried the same wallet for almost fifteen years and haven't paid much attention to the scraps crumbled deep inside the crevasses. That Post-it note about a woman who could interpret dreams strangely resurfaced when I was at the hospital. I'd misplaced my insurance card in the overstuffed cardholder of the beaten-up wallet and dumped out its contents on the counter at the surgery center at check-in. When the note landed face-up on the pile of junk, it startled me, but I couldn't hold up the line forming behind me to process its words and origin.

I was alone. Hospital visits had become so routine in our family that I drove myself to scheduled surgeries. The post-op nurses knew to call Brett on his cell phone when I made it to recovery to let him know how I was and whether or not I'd need to be admitted. If I had to spend the night, Brett and Simon would visit that evening after dinner. If I could be released, Brett had to drive me home because of the anesthesia. We always had the hassle of two cars to deal with. Sometimes I broke the rule and drove myself home, anyway. I didn't want my health to, once again, inconvenience Brett and Simon.

It was a couple days later when I remembered the note. I asked Simon about it when he came home from school and he vaguely recalled that he wrote it to save my place on the Kindle I was reading when I fell asleep in his bed. We pieced together that he had been around eight years old. At the time I had been captivated with *The Alchemist* by Paulo Coelho. It's the story about a shepherd boy named Santiago who goes on an epic journey to fulfill his dream: his "personal legend." Every couple of minutes, I'd interrupt Simon's own reading to give updates and share details about Santiago's adventures and how the entire universe conspired to help the little hero find his treasure. One of the first characters Santiago meets is an old gypsy woman, "the woman who could interpret his dreams." After the protagonist eagerly sought meaning from her on a recurring dream that compelled him on his quest, she simply encouraged him to stay on the journey and then charged him one-tenth of the treasure that she was sure he would find at the end. It was practical, non-flashy, mom-like advice with an expected return on investment at the end.

Our time reading *The Alchemist* inspired me to tell Simon to "sleep well and dream big like Santiago" every night before going to sleep.

That time is etched into his memory because I was sick and Brett was sad. We had just reluctantly completed the sale of our business to a local firm and were still grieving the loss of what we considered to be our dream, our personal legend. For five years, Brett and I owned and operated an advertising agency in downtown Milwaukee that made a lot of creative noise in the industry. At our peak, we had five full-time employees who were young, cool, and widely heralded up-and-comers. Business was going well, our work was winning awards and bringing us more work, and we had just retained a relocation firm to help find a new space for our anticipated expansion.

Brett and I had both worked in the advertising industry for fifteen years when we decided to go off on our own. I had been heavily involved with two industry-related startups prior to this and was ready to put what I had learned into practice for ourselves. Brett floated among several agencies and had ample opportunity to identify his preferred best practices based on the bits and pieces he picked up from other shops. It was his dream first: to own an agency at which he would be the CEO and call the shots. I enjoyed the thrill of starting up businesses and wanted to create something with my husband that would become our family's "legend."

A few short months after completing our expansion plans, our country would be in the midst of the worse economic disaster since the Great Depression of 1929. Prices plunged, the stock market crashed, and the housing market tanked. It felt like the world was in a free-fall, and we, as advertising agency owners, were staring straight into the abyss. Marketing budgets froze, projects dried up, and clients with signed contracts disappeared. Everyone contracted. We reversed course on our expansion and put all of our focus into saving the business and our people.

We would have made it, too, if only I hadn't become sick again. We had financial reserve and a diversified portfolio of clients to limp through payroll each month. What we didn't have was great health insurance and time for me to heal.

My health had been on the decline for nearly a year at that time. Since my Crohn's Disease diagnosis at age sixteen, I've had recurring bouts every few years. Every one of those bouts caused me a couple more feet of intestines and frequent flyer points in the emergency room. All the signs at the time were pointing to another full-blown bout on the horizon.

Crohn's is an auto-immune disease marked with intense symptoms of pain, malnutrition, and digestive disorders. Symptoms are often hastened by stress. As the economy slid, my imminent decline was exasperated. By the time we closed our agency, I was surviving on a feeding tube. My mind and body fogged out everything that made me who I was. I was empty and scared of what would become of us as a business, as a couple, and as a family.

The only thing that got me through that time was reading books with Simon. When we climbed into his bed together at night, I was grateful that I had made it through another day. We read and whispered and prayed together that the next day would be just a little better. He usually fell asleep first. I was sure to tell him to "sleep well and dream big like Santiago" before we started reading so those words would seep into his dreams.

For fourteen years, Simon and I read together nightly. He was an early reader and devoured chapter books by the time he was just seven. Sometimes we'd share a book aloud; most times we read different books side-by-side. I have read every single night of my life since college. With Simon to share it with, this became a beloved nightly ritual with me. His taste in books was sports fiction with a young protagonist who always found a way to overcome all odds to succeed on the field. I've read just about anything I could get my hands on in the last twenty-five years, with the exception of business books. I don't understand why people would sacrifice their precious imagination time at the end of a busy day with a series of "how-to's."

For nearly two more years after our first "Alchemist evening," I held onto my advertising agency career, despite full dependence on a feeding tube and severe immobility and complications due to malnutrition. I wasn't showing any signs of progress and our family was coming to terms with a potentially grim future. When discussions about bone marrow transplants started to gain traction among my care team, I knew that I had to make serious changes. The one thing I couldn't afford to do was stop working.

Instead, I found an open position at a private university near our suburban home. It wasn't an ideal position, but it allowed me an opportunity to get off the agency grind and truly focus on myself and my health. With a brand new dress and a scarf that hid my feeding tube, I went into the interview with a hopeful feeling that things were going to get better. Simon and I had used our reading time to pray together the night before.

When I was offered the job, I scheduled a start date for six weeks later to detangle myself from agency life and enter a thirty-five-day oxygen therapy program. This controversial treatment would involve me being locked in a hyperbaric chamber every day for the next month. A hyperbaric chamber looks like a giant test tube resting on its side. The top half opens, and you slide in snugly, like you would in a coffin if you were still alive. At all times you remain in full display of a nurse, which feels a little weird. There were two chambers in the room, so oftentimes I reclined next to someone else receiving treatment. We were a bit like resting mermaids, behind glass. These human vaults were equipped with video monitors so we could bring movies to help us pass the time and take our minds off being trapped. The entire treatment lasted about three hours; I couldn't just climb out if ever I felt uncomfortable because the chambers were pressurized, and a nurse was responsible for simulating ascension and descension for a safe exit. If I came up too fast, apparently my eardrums could explode, and I would get very sick.

I once witnessed a middle-aged man suffer a panic attack during his treatment. It was clearly his first treatment because he had a lot of questions and stalled before getting in. I couldn't hear him because I was already entombed, but I recognized his anxiety. After about a half hour I noticed some commotion from the next tube over in my peripheral vision. The man banged on his tube as he rocked from side-to-side with a crazed look on his face. His eyes appeared wide and bulgy—like that Chucky doll before slaughtering an unsuspecting teenager. The nurse did all she could do to soothe him from outside the glass until he was depressurized enough to be let out. When it was finally time, he leapt out of the tube, soaked and manic, and practically jumped his way to the exit door only pausing slightly to grab his slides. That started me on a panic. I was nearly finished with *Sideways*, the movie I'd brought, when his attack became contagious. When I got the nurses attention I signaled for her to begin my long evacuation and did what I could to remain calm.

In theory, the daily blast of oxygen would help my wounds and scar tissue heal. In the end, the treatment did not work, and I developed such intense feelings of loneliness and isolation from being locked into the small space that I embodied a sadness that made my limbs heavy and my thoughts desperate. Instead of feeling fresh for my new job, I was exhausted and battled with thoughts of giving up.

I thought my good days were behind me. I felt like a failure at work and that my dreams were dead. I couldn't envision a full, healthy future for myself or our family. My only concern was getting through the day so I could read with Simon at night, watch him drift off to sleep.

At the university, I found a team of coworkers who made me laugh and a work environment that encouraged me to pray. Nobody knew exactly what was happening to me, but they offered me grace as I found my way back to health. Every single day I noticed small signs of improvement, and, in time, they began celebrating little victories with me. While my productivity certainly improved at work, it was my energy and presence at home that was most appreciated.

I had finally come out of my latest bout of Crohn's; it wasn't my worst, and it certainly won't be my last. As the insidious creature hibernates deep inside me only to resurface more cunning in a couple years, I choose to make the most of my precious in-between time. In a moment of serendipity, I discovered the river at a time when I felt confident and strong enough to stand among those along the edge.

The way people fish along the river—together, but separately—reminds me of how Simon and I came together at night. We each silently read our own thing, but we were together in our own safe world doing it. There is no time I cherish more with my son than those nights reading before he fell asleep.

Simon doesn't talk about those days much. He remembers that they were long and hard, and that reading was about the only thing I could do with enthusiasm. As he prepares for college, I hope that he finds passions in life that he can share between himself and those he loves. I hope that he enters a career that will keep him motivated to work hard and laugh loudly with coworkers, through good and lean times. I hope that he's not afraid to take risks and learns from inevitable failures. Finally, I hope that he continues to find solace and comfort in books and escapes his own busy world for a while before going to bed at night. Sleep well and dream big, like Santiago.

CHAPTER FOUR

TOO LATE TO STOP NOW

Brett's palms itch every time he hears the sound of a race car. It is a symptom of longing that doesn't go away with time. At the age of thirty, Brett fulfilled his childhood dream of becoming a race car driver, and the thrill was even greater than he expected.

"Not everyone has the balls to drive 'hellafast' into the corner," he said with long-missing passion. "I wasn't sure I could do it at first, and then that adrenaline kicked in." For racers, a healthy dose of adrenaline doesn't necessarily make them go faster, but it does sharpen their focus.

"Bad things happen if you're not focused," he lectured. He then listed a number of things that drivers need to be aware of while controlling such powerful vehicles: when to break, where to hit a corner, and how to unwind into the straightway. "It starts with the eyes," he said. "Your hands drive you where your eyes go."

In his everyday life, Brett doesn't describe anything as "hella," and often refers to guys who compare balls as "meatheads." Now, he hasn't raced in almost a decade and since then has been personally dented in some tough life corners.

His macho swagger only resurfaces when he recalls his racing days at Road America.

Road America, "America's National Park of Speed," is a four-mile road course carved into the hills of Wisconsin's Kettle Moraine. It has fourteen different turns and is considered by many in racing to be one of the best road courses in the world. It opened in 1955 and had captured Brett's imagination ever since he was kid in the 1970s. He only officially raced a handful of times, but he took lessons at the track's driving school, and spent several summers hanging around the pits just to pick up a second-hand buzz.

"Road America is a different world," described Brett. "Nowhere else are fans allowed the kind of access that they're allowed there. We could spend the day at the track and get up close in the corners and then walk among the teams and their pits in between races. That kind of exposure was exhilarating to me as a kid...It still is."

We didn't own a race car. As a graduate of the open-wheel driving school, Brett could pay to use one in the class fleet. Open wheel cars are simply cars, but with wheels outside the main body instead of below the body or fenders. With his signature, we assumed all risk of injury to driver and car. At each race, I resumed my usual spot at corner number five so I could see him coming in and going out on long, fast stretches. He was clipped a couple times during his short career, but no scares or bumps permanently scratched his itch for more.

Brett's fire suit, a blue and silver flame-resistant onesie, made his tall lean frame even longer. He'd strut like Travolta when he wore it, with the top half down and tied around his waist.

A coworker of mine once described Brett as "an elegant man." Twenty years later, and he still earns that description.

He is six-foot-two-inches tall, has a full head of blonde hair, piercing blue eyes, a chiseled jawline, and maintains a lean, swimmer's body frame—even at forty-nine years old. He has such a striking look that strangers often stop him to comment on his appearance and physical demeanor. Most commonly, they point out his posture.

Brett is physical proof that sitting up straight and carrying one's self proudly will command respect and attention. The guys who worked with us at our agency actually nicknamed him "Posture" in jest. It usually went something like, "What's up, Posture!" His walk is distinct and admirable; it adds to his elegance.

Brett and I were high school sweethearts. We were both sixteen on our first date to the movies, back in 1988. We went to different high schools and were in different grades, but we fell for each other by staying upright as competitive downhill skiers. "Competitive" is a generous description for what it was we actually did. Brett and his friends started a ski team their senior year in high school and there were more administrative gates to pass than any of them expected. The team's first year was rough, and we members did more scrambling and organizing than actual racing. By the second year, my senior year, our team was more established, with official uniforms and proper coaching, and we actually won a couple meets.

We were casual daters at first. I wasn't feeling well and, outside of skiing, spent most nights and weekends at home. My friends drifted away during that time, but Brett came in closer. During skiing's off-season, Brett was a competitive swimmer and had late swim practice most nights of the week. Since my house was halfway between the pool and his home, he made a habit of stopping by on his way to or from. The smell of chlorine still makes me tingly inside.

Brett was a good-looking kid who drove a black Turbo Saab and kept mainly to himself. He was liked and included but remained mostly a mystery to the girls in town. When he started opening up around me and my family, I felt honored, trusted, and chosen. He could have been with any girl and he chose me—the fun girl with a great family and a weird bowel disease.

We navigated the distance between our colleges, in Chicago and Milwaukee, with the help of Amtrak and took turns hopping the rails to visit each other on weekends. When I was just nineteen, he surprised me with a ring at a family dinner during Thanksgiving weekend. He graduated from college a year before I did and moved to Milwaukee so we could plan our wedding and start our lives.

Surrounded by our family and friends, many of whom were involved in the Milwaukee music scene, Brett and I said our vows in the Catholic Church where I was raised. Then we threw a party complete with a keg in the corner and a ballroom full of broke young adults who knew how to cut loose. The night was a blur to us, but when we danced to our song, "Into the Mystic" by Van Morrison, we were fully aware of the commitment we had just made to each other. The last line of the song is, "too late to stop now," and we shouted those words convincingly into each other's smiling, sweaty faces, and meant it.

One year into our marriage, Brett had to make a life-or-death call on my behalf. I was passed out cold on a hospital bed in severe toxicity due to peritonitis that started in my colon. My Crohn's had acted up again. The doctors needed permission to cut me open and remove the damage in my colon. They warned Brett that they might not be able to stitch me back together right away, or even at all. He had little choice but to agree to proceed. A few anxious hours later, I was wheeled back to my room packed with tubes, jars, and the dreaded colostomy bag. I was a groggy mess; he was relieved.

I learned to get good at poker during my long stay in the hospital. With the high stakes of hard candy on the line, nurses, doctors, friends and family spent time teaching me the nuances of the game and, eventually, shared their best winning secrets. My friends made it a sport to feed me red Jolly Ranchers just to watch my stomach drainage jars turn bright red. They even took overs-and-unders on the time it would take. Brett was by my side so often that he learned to change my IV bags, reset my double pumps, and refasten the steri-strips that held my guts in place. He could do all these things without putting down his ham sandwich.

Weeks later, I prepared to finally leave the hospital. To help us adjust to our new life with a colostomy bag, a nurse walked us through cleaning and changing procedures. Brett had to be there, too. Following the demonstration, we had to watch a video about how to enjoy sex with a colostomy. That was the first time that I cried. We had been so busy tracking my progress, that it never occurred to us (or at least me) how that part of our married life would change. The people in the video were ugly. Their descriptions were gross. And they tried too hard to convince us that they still had desires for each other. We weren't convinced.

The next day, we packed me up and hobbled to the car in my first flash of fresh air in almost three weeks. To our surprise, those months with a colostomy were among our happiest. We did all the things that were difficult for me in the past. We enjoyed large crowds at festivals and concerts; we stood in long lines to go on scary roller coasters at theme parks; we went on epic road trips without tracking the bathroom stops; and we enjoyed carefree outings with our friends from Marquette. When my doctors determined that I was healthy enough to be reattached, we were rather reluctant.

Brett is infuriatingly good at most things. I think the term for people like him is "polymath." He can golf, bowl, bat, cook, drive, write, and fix stuff that's broken. With so many natural gifts, he rarely had to work hard to master a new skill. We make a good team because I'm scrappy, rough around the edges, and impatient; he is measured, smooth, and cautious. His calm demeanor can be mistaken for aloofness. Even I get fooled at times.

He worked in retail in Chicago through college and stayed with the same company when he moved to Milwaukee. He is really good at caring for people and gets energized when he can help them solve problems. He bounced around in similar positions for some years before landing a job in advertising, where we worked alongside one another. I had recently left my event job at a major tourist attraction to try my hand at an agency. I had only been there one month when I introduced my young husband to the bosses. Despite having no real advertising experience, they hired Brett on the spot. Probably his excellent posture had a lot to do with that solid first impression.

That started his journey in advertising, one that would lead him on commercial sets across the country and propel us to open our own award-winning agency years later. The day we sold our business was the last day that Brett proudly and confidently spoke about his career and our chosen industry. That was nine years ago. Brett has since bounced around in a number of positions until landing happily, in full-circle, back into retail and helping people.

As a kid, he fished for trout on the end of his grandparents' pier on a large body of water toward the center of the state. He learned to fish from his dad and grandfather and hoped that he could extend that tradition with Simon. When Simon was really young, Brett purchased two poles and a basic tackle kit in anticipation of a father-son outing. They never went. Those poles sat unused in our garage.

Brett likes that I'm learning to fish. When I first talked with him about it, he compared fishing to racing. "The actual hooking of a fish is extremely exhilarating, just like racing," he said. He went on to add, "Both rely on technique, intuition, skill, and problem-solving." Although, unlike racing, he concedes that fishing also relies on patience and a high degree of luck.

The number one question he gets asked about my fishing is how he "lets" me go into invisible places in the city with unknown people, mostly men. In our thirty-plus years of being together, I have never sought permission from him, and he has never assumed he was in a position to grant it. Even though we were just teenagers when we started out, he knew exactly what he was getting into when he asked me to marry him. Growing up, my grandmothers were the tough ones who kept our family close and in check. One, Cecilia, the farmer's wife, was a role model of hard work and perseverance. She also had a quick wit and used colorful language to get her message across. The other, Mrs. Cody, was proper, cultured, educated, and worldly; she demanded that her granddaughters were ladies in her presence. She, in particular, loved Brett for his manners and his posture.

My mom is tough like her farmer mom. Her daughters are educated, driven, and indivisible. We know how to work hard, speak with an edge, and stand our ground in heels. Together, we have always been an impenetrable little force of nature that the men who love us understand.

For my birthday this year, Brett bought me my very own tackle box, with built-in pockets for snacks. He also designed a t-shirt with the word "Fortitude" on the front in earnest recognition of how hard I work and how proud of me he is. When I wear it under a jacket just the letters "t i t" are visible, which makes me giggle. I love the shirt and his unintentional statement. I love him for creating it for me. He sees the good in me and supports me unconditionally. We've had some tough days, but both of us adhere to the words we screamed recklessly into each other's faces on our wedding night: "It's too late to stop now."

CHAPTER FIVE

WATCH WHERE YOU HOOK

———

My first solo cast, on a hell-hot day in July, hooked my pants. They were slouchy gray sweatpants with a drawstring, so the potential for a tear was high. These pants were supposed to mask my age, which was forty-eight, and help me blend into the crowd, which was predictably all-male and quite diverse. While I fooled no one—women my age don't fish in the city— it helped me to feel unnoticed. Disguised.

No matter how I dressed, I stood out because I was alone and a rookie. A true rookie. I had never even caught a fish.

So, what's a middle-aged woman doing by herself at the Milwaukee River with a fishing pole? It certainly wasn't for the fish. I hate fish. I don't even like visiting aquariums to look at fish. I never enjoyed swimming with any fish or water creature, especially in waters that camouflaged their existence. I have lived in Wisconsin, the state that holds Friday Fish Fry sacred, my entire life and I've never even tried to eat fish. During Lent, the forty days before Easter, Wisconsin residents leave work early on Fridays just to get to a restaurant in time to eat that same night. Every man, woman, and child eats fried fish on Fridays. You could plan a home robbery around it. This holy ritual is one in which I have never partaken. Even I don't understand my defiance on that count.

The Friday Fish Fry is a weekly community event in every small bar, restaurant, and hall in the state. The ritual came to Wisconsin with the Catholics from Ireland, Poland, and Germany. Their practice was to not eat meat on Fridays, and fish was not considered proper meat. Fish here were also easy and cheap, and the practice of frying allowed for high-volume preparation. Traditional servings include beer-batter, coleslaw, potato pancakes, and marble rye bread. The meal is usually precluded with a Brandy Old-Fashioned Sweet and topped off with a Miller pint. For non-fish eaters like me, establishments usually offer a roasted chicken with fries option, but the fries share the same oil vat as the pervasive fish. We must, after all, be flexible.

Without articulating it at the time, I went down to the river to discover my "after"—that thing I was actually searching for—under the ruse of doing something else. Thoreau wrote about it famously in *Walden*. He wrote about how men could fish their whole lives for reasons other than catching fish.

I started fishing to get to know the people and their stories, to learn what they were actually after. Even though Thoreau was specific to men, I related to his sentiments and was eager to dabble in my own version of Walden Pond. I wanted to discover what I might learn from the men who were there faithfully and from my experience of trying something new in unknown surroundings with people with whom I seemingly had nothing in common.

Admittedly, this was a disconnect that would require a transformation in me and the help of many strangers.

Once, when I was around six, my family rented a cabin in northern Wisconsin with another family. For a full week, five kids shared two bamboo fishing poles, one pier, a rowboat, and a bedroom. The bamboo poles were too long for us at about six-feet tall. They simply had lines and bobbers tied around the ends; no hooks. We took turns tea-bagging the bobbers into the water, but with nothing to snag our prey, we only attracted attention and crowds of fish below the pier.

When not fighting over the poles, the other kids swam with the swarms of taunting fish who could sense the absence of hooks above. I stayed on the pier at a safe distance from any possible fish invasions. I kept busy choreographing song and dance numbers.

As a kid I liked to organize shows for our neighborhood. They were nothing more than convincing the other kids on the block to dance to songs that I themed together using my record player. There was a *Grease*-themed performance that coincided with the movie release. An *Endless Summer* show to the Beach Boys' album of the same name. And a *"Twist"* night that had each kid in the neighborhood perform solo hip thrusts to the song by Chubby Checker. I was the producer, promoter, performer, and technician who dropped the needle on the record. The adults in the neighborhood used these silly shows as an opportunity to drink beer together and eat chips and cheese. These were the can't-miss events of the season.

My favorite song that summer at the cabin was an instructive piece about how to make a peanut butter and jelly sandwich. I prepared an interpretive dance routine that I intended to teach the others for a surprise performance on our last day. In a flash spin move, I kicked both poles and my left red tennis shoe into the water. The poles floated but my shoe sank to the bottom of the shallow lake. The sinking red shoe attracted a school of minnows to investigate the unusual vessel. I watched as they swam in and around my shoe. Even though we eventually rescued the shoe, I went barefoot the rest of the trip.

It probably isn't fair to associate fish with losing a shoe, but, whatever. It gave my preexisting weird idiosyncrasy about fish an actual reason. What mattered was having an incident I could point to explain my aversion to fish.

If there are three things you know about Milwaukee, they are likely motorcycles, beer, and cheese. The culmination of these three things always, always comes back to Summerfest. I'm not sure when it was last verified, but Summerfest is billed as the world's largest music festival. For ten days in July, every touring band in the world stops through our city. Around a million people each year visit the beautiful festival grounds on the shores of Lake Michigan and eat fried cheese, drink Miller Beer, and see all their favorite bands.

When Summerfest is done, the festivals, fried cheese, and beer rolls on. Nearly every nationality claims their own weekend on the grounds. Add to that the State Fair, street festivals, neighborhood block parties, free music nights in the parks, farmers markets, and Milwaukee Brewers games, and there is little time to take up a new hobby, especially something as quiet as fishing.

Wisconsin winters are the stuff of legends. The windchill off Lake Michigan can plunge a crisp, bright afternoon into a darkness that sucks the air from your chest, freezes it mid-vapor, and then pounds your face with it like you're a walking hailstorm. It is so cold that dog leashes freeze into sculptures, driveways crack, and power lines buckle. Schools actually close in Wisconsin because of the cold. Our state became a viral sensation last year when locals threw buckets of colored water in the air to freeze into rainbows. Here, we buy hats and gloves to match our pajamas.

Our winters last through spring and finally leave with a near-summer rapid thaw that brings all our water sources to the brink. But there's always a spring teaser. That particular teaser, in March, introduced me to the underground world of urban fishing and hooked me into a secret culture and community that welcomed this white, middle-aged lady with open nets.

Despite the fact that my one-and-only fishing lesson was without a hook, I was eager to get out there. I chose a hot Saturday in July as my first official solo outing, hook and all. While we Wisconsinites take great pride in bragging about our winters, the temperature extremity is actually matched by our stifling hot and humid summers. On the day I decided to make my solo fishing debut, the temperature had already climbed to ninety degrees and weathermen were advising everyone to drink water, stay indoors, and check on our elderly neighbors.

It was the kind of day that compelled people to cancel their plans. Nevertheless, the river was hopping because it was Saturday. No weather will stop urban fishermen from being out by the river on that one sacred day of the week. As a new urban fisher, I too stuck to my plans.

Seven people were already lined up when I arrived. Three of them were "fondue fishing." You know what I'm talking about. A bunch of guys standing in a semi-circle sword-fighting their poles like hungry people at a seventies-styled party with long forks, a fiery pot of bubbling chocolate, and a pile of cake chunks in the center. If the cake survives the chocolate dip, it will most certainly burn the roof of your mouth.

Despite the fire and the burn, I chose chocolate fondue at my birthday parties when I was a kid. It made me feel sophisticated. Danger wasn't a thing; we'd kabob our forks with cherries, cake, marshmallows, and pineapple, and elbowed and shoved our friends aside to get the first, fullest dip of brown lava. We'd over-heap our forks to the point that the chocolate trailed from table to carpet to shoes to shirt before scorching our taste buds. Over time, we learned to tarp the floor. We never learned to let it cool.

We had chunks of cake; my river mates had lures and minnows.

The fondue fishermen huddled together so closely that their bobbers practically touched, yet they never uttered a word.

I reminded myself to keep quiet and blend. In addition to my gray drawstrings, I wore a gender neutral blue NFL t-shirt, dirty Adidas tennis shoes, and a black trucker hat to complete my wallflower look. It was so hot, a line of sweat started at my cleavage and trickled down to my stomach. My visible and dreaded boob sweat negated any chance I had for appearing non-binary.

A young boy stood shin-deep in the rolling water at the top of the falls. He held his pole in one hand and scrolled his phone with the other.

Also at the bank was an African American man in his late forties who wore a blue Superman t-shirt, gray Adidas athletic pants, red Nikes, and a green baseball hat with the Milwaukee Bucks logo. He sat on a paint bucket while enjoying a Miller Lite, with evidence that this was not his first of the day. He is a Saturday regular, and while we've never spoken, we smiled and nodded to each other in mutual recognition. I tried to recall if I've ever seen him reel in a fish.

Two teenage boys I hadn't seen before crowded in on Superman's territory. I planted myself a safe distance from them and awkwardly readied my gear. Over the rolling sound of the falls, I could faintly hear that the boys spoke in Spanish to each other. I think they were talking about ice cream.

There wasn't an opportunity for the customary fishing greeting. "How're they biting today?" one would ask.

"Ah-right," another would respond.

It would soon come in handy that the phrase, "Excuse me, but would you help me pull this hook out of my backside?" is universally understood using other methods of communication.

I was fresh off a practice cast in my backyard. We'd had those two fishing poles and small, cobwebby tackle box hiding in our garage for at least a decade. One was still strung from the summer that Simon tried fishing camp; the other had never been unwrapped. The fully-strung one, called The Ugly Stik, had a weighted, lime green lure with a jiggly tail meant to simulate swimming in the water to attract curious fish. To me, it's a giant gummy fish with bulging eyes. The stick and the gummy fish were to be the tools for my inaugural cast.

In my backyard that morning, Brett, who enjoyed fishing when he was a kid, gave me a few pointers. Our property has nearly a full acre of grass surrounded by trees. He and I stood together in the middle of the yard and he agreed to demonstrate how the whole contraption worked. His first cast, a beautiful twenty-yard, one-handed sidearm, got caught in a tree, which was remarkable because there was only one tree hazard in our vicinity. When it was my turn, my cast (a two-handed side) went about four feet in front of me. Since I managed to avoid all surrounding obstacles, we called it a success.

That one backyard cast was my only experience. Despite being thoroughly unprepared, I took a swig of whiskey for courage, packed my gummy fish and pole, and headed toward the river blasting "Jack Straw" by the Grateful Dead on my car radio.

Jack Straw from Wichita
Cut his buddy down
Dug for him a shallow grave
And laid his body down

I was really nervous. I sat in my car for one more Dead song, "Truckin'," to settle my flipping stomach. What the hell was I even thinking? How would the community of mostly men respond to a woman entering their silent world uninvited and with absolutely no qualifications to be there in the first place?

In my narrow confines between the boys speaking Spanish and some trees, I tried my first ever two-handed overhead cast. I envisioned that I was a pitcher with tight precision and body control on the mound staring down my opponent. But my form was less a punishing fastball and more bad-lumber-jack-hacking-an-ax. I paused. Kept my eyes on the spot in the river where I wouldn't get tangled with other lines and trees. I pictured my body naturally torqueing with excellent follow-through. I raised my arms, probably too high, and went for it. I karate-chopped my first overhand cast into the river, near the falls on a busy Saturday morning.

Only, I flicked my wrist. With that small flick of my wrist, my line swung down behind me and the bulging-eyed jelly fishhook caught my pants.

If you don't know, fishing hooks are sharp. They're sharp enough to embed into the mouths of fish upon a quick engagement; sharp enough to embed into a pair of drawstring sweatpants. Being unaware of my "catch," I continued the follow-through and stayed focused on where I wanted my hook to land: in the water.

It happened so fast. At the same time that my backside tugged, my right arm caught, but my body kept moving forward. A potential flesh wound was not my biggest worry, however. It was the potential of face-planting into the river that required my immediate attention.

My "oh no" squeal was my only hope for help. Superman looked over first, but the boys had faster reflexes. One handed his pole to the other and grabbed my arms enough to stabilize me. This small gesture stopped my momentum and caused me to drop my pole.

Clearly, the line was still attached to my rear.

I tried to see where, exactly, but my neck didn't bend that far back. I managed to avoid a Benny Hill moment chasing my own backside in double-time to the tune of "Yakety Sax" and, instead, just stood still and locked eyes with the kid. We shared a nod and then I turned around so he could have a good look at the situation. His small smirk was more of understanding than condemnation—like he'd given himself a good hook before too. With little ceremony and no words, he pulled it out.

I knew the others saw what happened. I wanted them to know that I was in on the joke. I recognized that this was a funny story: a fish story that would only get better with time.

So, I broke the silence.

"Did you all see that?"

They did.

"At least I caught something!" I said while avoiding all eye contact.

Superman, still sitting on his bucket, let out a jovial "hah hee" laugh and raised his Miller Lite in my direction. He made eye contact and smiled. And then he said something to me that was so friendly, so oddly welcoming into his fraternity, so human, that I knew I would come back and try it again.

"What kinda cast was that?" he asked, shaking his head. "Unless there's a fish in your ass, don't hook it."

CHAPTER SIX

MAN ON THE STREAK

———

I had no desire to be "one with nature" when I set out to learn to fish. My motivation was quite the opposite. I saw the quiet, comfortable way that people of all races, backgrounds, and ages interacted with each other while doing something they loved; I wanted to be alongside them. A week after my lesson with Keith and my pants fiasco, I mustered up the courage to go back down to the dam to try again. To my surprise, I was the only one there. It hadn't rained in a while and the once-flowing river was reduced to a trickle with rock hazards along the bottom, just waiting for a rookie fisher to stick her hook.

On one hand, being alone allowed me an opportunity to work out my awkward cast and switch flick motion without fear of hooking a bystander. It also gave me private time to visualize the sequence of button, line, release…button, line, release…without judgement. Fishermen might not say much, but they are always quietly watching each other. On the other hand, it meant that when I inevitably got my hook stuck in a rock a few feet in stream, there was no one there to help me get it out.

It happened on my fourth cast: a solid effort with a good arc, at a respectable distance. I let it sit out there the obligatory time I guessed it would take to drum up business from curious bass down below. I watched my bobber bounce and weave, bounce and weave in mesmerizing rhythm on the lazy, shallow banks of the river.

When I reeled it in to do it again, I felt a tug from below that arched my pole. At first I thought I had hooked something big. I wrestled my taut line back and forth as if I was in a duel with a king salmon. I ground my reel left and right to make the line as tight as possible. When it seemed like my pole was about to crack from the pressure, I realized my hook was stuck.

It was an embarrassing time for my solitude to be broken. I was unsuccessfully negotiating my hook from the rock when a good-looking man with brown skin and a huge smile practically trotted toward me. He wore a baseball hat and kept his sunglasses over the bill like a cool teenager. He had on an orange t-shirt, black work pants, and shoes that gave the appearance that he was coming or going to a job. His speed and lack of gear struck me. He carried only a pole and walked with a purpose, like he had places to be. In quick stride and without a greeting, the man put his pole down, walked upright down the rocky bluff, gracefully jumped from rock to rock, and bent down in the water to loosen my hook. He stayed dry the entire time.

He didn't wait for me to express my appreciation. Instead, he walked back up the bluff easily and went right to the task at hand: catch a fish in the next thirty minutes. "Are they biting today?" he asked without waiting for my reply. He crouched down low and close to the dams, side-dunked his hook into the water, and jiggled and bounced his short line about a foot from shore before looking back up at me and invitingly asking again, "Any bites?"

I would later learn that this crouching, waving style is referred to as jigging. Jigging is the practice of fishing with a type of reel that covers the hook with soft, brightly-colored material that, when jiggled, is meant to resemble a fish swimming.

Angel Perez, Junior, is an urban fishing streaker. He makes at least one cast in a Milwaukee watering hole every single day of the year. That morning, he stopped by the park on the way to his maintenance job at a hotel a few miles away. He had to move fast because he barely left himself enough time to cast, yet alone make a catch. Seven months (209 days, precisely) into the year, and he'd caught a fish on all but three of those days. He had the selfies to prove it.

He introduced himself to me and handed me his phone, with a cracked screen, so I could see for myself. He remained crouched at the side of the falls; I sat down on the rocks next to him and scrolled through his hundreds of pictures. We were close together so that we could share the cracked screen on the sunny day.

"Your finger won't get cut," he said when I scrolled too gingerly. "There's a screen protector so go on and look!" He really wanted me to see his pictures.

I used one of my hands to shield the sun from the mosaic screen and still had to squint to see picture after picture of him and fish. In the next thirty minutes, I learned a lot about my new friend—and noticed that he has a good side when it comes to posing for pictures.

"The best thrill is when you catch a fish and someone is there to take your picture," he said to me while shifting his attention back and forth between his phone in my hand

and his hook in the water. "There's a certain way you hold it for your picture." He put his pole down for just a second to demonstrate by placing his hands in a position of offering at church—elbows bent, palms up in front about chest high.

I stopped my scrolling on a good close-up of him with a fish, perfectly displayed like he'd described. "You see?" he asked and pointed to the picture. "You want to show the fish, Leeza. Show the colors. The color came out nice on that one because I had my flash." It also came out nicely because he was shot from up top and slightly from the east, so that the sun formed a halo around his tilted-to-one-side face. The random stranger who captured his catch that day clearly had some photo skills.

Angel's daily fishing ritual was inspired from his youth in Chicago, where he lived with his dad in the shadows of Wrigley Field. He was born in the Bronx, the only child to his Puerto Rican parents in a bilingual working class apartment. His dad was an orchestra singer and maintenance man, and his mom kept up the apartment. He is proud to be an American citizen and is pleased his journey led him to Milwaukee.

"This is the greatest country on earth, Leeza," he declared. "I love America and all our freedoms!"

Like "Jenny from the Block," Angel describes himself as Nuyorican, a term for Puerto Ricans born or raised in New York City. He often says that he was "born in the Bronx, grew up in Chicago, but Milwaukee is his home." Angel and his father moved to Chicago for employment opportunities after his parents got divorced, when Angel was six years old. Like his dad, Angel is a hard worker and is good with his hands, so he could always find work. Angel's dad was a manager in manufacturing, but his real passion was singing.

While Angel is bilingual, he and his dad prefer to speak in Spanglish, using combinations of words or phrases from both their cultures. His accent isn't easily detected, but his speaking mannerisms are unique for Wisconsin. For example, as soon as I told him my name, he used it. Often. And he pronounces it with a hard emphasis on the "e" and "z" sounds.

"What do you think about this, Leeza?"

"Leeza, you'll get a fish yet!"

"Just you wait, Leeza. I'll help you get there!"

A prolific baseball player, Angel managed to stay out of trouble by participating in Little League. He was an offensive slugger who played third base and catcher. When he and his teammates weren't playing baseball, they biked to open water to fish. They kept their bat bags and their fishing rods attached to their bikes, so they could seamlessly pursue both passions during those endless summer days. He continued playing ball for various sponsored leagues in Chicago and in Milwaukee after he moved.

Angel is a city boy drawn to natural water sources. As a teenager, he became a lifeguard at a Chicago public beach and was even recognized as Rookie of the Year his first year for making a few high profile rescues. When he wasn't sitting in his guard chair, he'd escape to a quiet part of the city's public waters to get a cast in.

He enjoyed school and was a good student. He's proud of the fact that he still keeps in touch with a few of his childhood classmates, including the young woman who would become his wife. Upon graduation, Angel started his maintenance career, married his high school sweetheart, and had two children—a boy and a girl. He and his wife raised their family in the city, and Angel was able to share his passions for urban fishing and baseball with them.

"My family is a good family. I never want to bring any shame or disrespect to them," said Angel. "I always try to act in a way that brings them honor."

After a divorce, Angel moved to Milwaukee where a maintenance position waited for him. His son moved to Milwaukee soon after. His ex-wife and daughter remained in Chicago, but Angel stayed in close contact with them, despite living in separate cities. They relied on the train for frequent visits. Eventually his daughter also relocated to Milwaukee. His kids had their own kids, and now Angel is a proud grandfather of five. Angel and his ex-wife remain in contact. On the day we met, he showed me a picture of his youngest granddaughter Mimi, from a birthday party taken the day before. He says she is beautiful just like his ex-wife.

Angel's father remained in Chicago and remarried a woman that Angel lovingly refers to as a "hillbilly." To him, that is not a derogatory word. "My step-mom was an actual hillbilly from the hills of Kentucky," confirmed Angel. Their marriage blended two seemingly opposite cultures and people together in highly influential and enjoyable ways for Angel. For example, he likes "hillbilly music" and gave Johnny Cash as an example.

It was nearly time for Angel to leave for work. Neither of us wanted to break up our conversation. Finally, on his last, last cast I found the nerve to ask him if he would teach me to fish. That's when he made one final revelation to me that would seal our friendship and add a greater purpose to our future fishing adventures together. When Angel retires in five years, his dream is to run an urban fishing charter business in Milwaukee so he could maintain his daily streak and share his love of fishing with others while introducing them to favorite spots in his beloved city.

It was settled. He would help me learn to fish. I would be his first customer. Our serendipitous meeting left both of us excited for our first official outing. We made plans to meet again in two days. Like Angel, I, too, am inexplicably committed to a couple of every-single-day habits. Of all the things we bonded over, our mutual obsession with maintaining a rigorous daily streak was our most profound. On the day of our meeting, I had clocked in my 410th day of working out thirty minutes or more in a row and hadn't missed a night of reading in nearly twenty-five years.

Inadvertently, we are poster children for the 365 Project, or any one of the hundreds of blogs and books dedicated to the daily habits of people. Successful people, happy people, optimistic people, healthy people, wealthy people, productive people…all of them, according to the internet, have one thing in common: a daily streak. It's not you, it's your routine that could be preventing you from living your wildest dreams.

A 365-day project started as an online photo challenge where photographers at every skill level challenged themselves to take a photo every day for a year and post it to any one of the sites dedicated to this trend. Often, there are themes attached to keep people participating year after year. The idea of a daily challenge has since expanded to deeds and actions. Some people declare they'll write nightly in a journal, others commit to thanking at least one person every day. The list of dailies is unending. Angel with his fishing and me with daily exercise and reading are unwittingly on trend.

My reading habit started in college. I couldn't sleep, didn't have cable, and the internet wasn't a personal thing yet, so there wasn't much else to occupy my anxious overnight hours. Since then, I've learned to savor my sleeplessness with books and have been on a lifelong, obsessive independent study journey ever since. I've created several themes for myself over the years. One year I dedicated solely to biographies. Another year, I read nothing but books on World War II. Then there was the strange year that I tackled the "M" shelf at my favorite bookstore, and only read books written by authors whose last name started with the letter "M." Finally, my most productive use of insomnia was when I decided to relearn French during the *oui* hours of the night. If there's any theme I'm following now, its fiction in the section marked, "popular for book clubs."

As for working out, it's all or nothing for me. It's either programmed into my daily routine, or it doesn't happen. I started it because a number of my fun friends were doing it and I wanted to spend more time with them, but I stuck with it because I could feel myself getting stronger and healthier. The more I did, the more I *did*. And the more confident and stronger I became.

Confidence and strength are blessings to me. Working out has become my daily badge of defiance against my disease and the hopeless thoughts that once filled my head. My mornings on the mat help me look ahead, not just for the day but for forever. There was a time when things were so dark that I could only hope for another night to read with Simon. Now, I'm able to look beyond nightly reading and beyond when Simon leaves home. I have an opportunity and the strength to try something entirely new and all by myself. For now, with my new friend Angel's help, that something new is fishing.

CHAPTER SEVEN

JUST ENOUGH
IS ENOUGH

———

Gypsy Geoff will be the first to tell you he's not your average birthday clown. He's a wise-cracking, nomadic street performer who has won international busking competitions and hustled on streets in Ireland, New Orleans, and San Francisco. He's a classically-trained chef and foodie who has spent nearly a decade "singing for his supper" at festivals across America. He tracks his favorite restaurants on an app and knows just where to eat when he makes it big on the pitch.

A pitch is the term used to describe an area that a busker has staked out and claimed for a performance. His self-proclaimed pitch on North Avenue is where Geoff and I first met in 2007, on Milwaukee's East Side at a daylong music festival a couple blocks east of the Milwaukee River. Geoff makes an art out of popping in and out of cities and lives. This vagabond who juggles and busks his way around the world offers rich lessons on self-reliance, living in the moment, and self-worth that have stuck with me long after his clown bus rolls on to his next stop.

The East Side is Milwaukee's stew of music, culture, and food. Hipsters, hippies, college students, and professionals converge in this area bordered by Lake Michigan, downtown, the University of Wisconsin Milwaukee, and the Milwaukee River on the West Side. The main artery of the East Side is North Avenue, a well-traveled thoroughfare that connects Lake Michigan with the rest of the city.

When I was a college student, Milwaukee's East Side was my home. Brett and I fell hard for the city's gritty live music scene. It was the early 1990s and the dawn of grunge. Seattle was still just a whisper. Bands like Nirvana and Pearl Jam were getting airplay on alternative stations. The heavy guitar *chenga, chenga, chenga,* and the rebel growl breaking through on the radio was a familiar sound to us Milwaukeeans who crawled the music bars on North Avenue on weeknights to avoid the five dollar weekend cover. What was soon-to-be dubbed grunge music from the Pacific coast was the kind of music we had been listening to in Milwaukee for years. That sexy, sweaty lumberjack look with the long hair and flannels? That's effortlessly, unironically ours, too.

Brett and I were involved with a couple bands back then. One we managed and the others couch surfed in our living room on rotation. These musicians were on the cusp, so close to making it that the *maybe* in the air was palpable. They avoided leases, quit jobs, and limited their possessions so they could be road-ready. They were all just getting by and our apartment was the only permanence in their otherwise in-between lives.

Milwaukee's moment never really came. Seattle's exciting music scene ran out of bands. Musicians died. Fans died. Grunge became a depressing symbol for heroin and slackers. While the rest of the nation moved on to bubblegum pop, we still clung to our heavy, dirty Milwaukee sound. Eventually the bands that we Pennie-Laned moved on. Some moved away and others found day jobs and responsible lives. Milwaukee still has a thriving music scene, but there isn't the same cohesive sound.

Fifteen years after our groupie days, I was hired to plan the East Side's twelve-hour music festival named Summer Soulstice. Because of our advertising agency, we had a solid grasp on pop culture and all things cool. We had beer, vodka, nacho cheese, bars, grocery, and higher education among our clients. It was our pulse on the ground and firm grasp of MySpace and emerging platform Facebook that got the attention of event organizers and clients trying to tap millennials' pockets. Backed by an agency full of cool creatives in their twenties, we were ready to build an experience on a blocked street canvas where fifteen thousand people would want to come and let loose.

From noon to midnight on the Saturday, closest to the longest day of the year, Milwaukeeans of all races, backgrounds, and ages shed their sweaters and bring their doughy winter bodies to the East Side. Soulstice's footprint includes three major stages, bike ramps for aerial BMX showcases, a dodge ball cage, food trucks, vendor tents, miniature golf, a DJ and dance floor, and bars. Lots and lots of bars.

Between dodge ball heats and BMX demonstrations, a young man wearing a tan wool vest and trousers and a green derby hawked in the street with the corner of a chair balanced on his chin. His street name was Gyspy Geoff, and he'd rolled into Soulstice from New Orleans to gauge Milwaukee's festival vibe and our cultural tolerance for street performers.

He managed to crack jokes with passersby while keeping the chair on his chin like it was just an outgrowth affixed to his cranium—no big deal. People stopped and engaged. He was funny and he had a chair on his chin. Geoff coaxed around three dozen people to sit down on the dirty blacktop in the middle of the hot day to see what more this guy with the chair on his face could do.

By the time I reached the scene to kick him out, too many people were invested. I was booed. I played it cool and approached the situation from a pragmatic angle. With a clipboard, I asked him for his insurance. All other performers at the festival had to sign waivers and produce documents that would exempt me from any liability. If they fell off the stage, got slapped with a dodge ball, or choked on a brat, I was not responsible. To my surprise, he was fully insured and had the documents to prove it. Without any more recourse, I sat down and watched the show with the others.

He full-body juggled gracefully using his hands, head, and feet. For a fleeting moment in Geoff's youth, he had aspired to become a professional hacky-sack athlete, so his hand-foot-eye coordination was on point. He used up all his cash to get to Milwaukee, and that didn't scare him. Geoff had always relied on the kindness of strangers and his own wits to get by. When that didn't work, he had fishing to keep him sustained. He always keeps his pole in his car.

Milwaukee is not particularly known for a thriving street performance scene. Beach cities and those with good public transportation tend to be more attractive. Cities like Key West, New Orleans, New York, San Francisco, Washington, D.C., and Los Angeles are at the top. Overseas, Scotland, Ireland, and England have the most visible street hustle.

"That vagabond life seemed romantic to me when I was a kid," says Geoff. "I wanted to be out on the streets in New

Orleans because those who were living on the edge fascinated me."

Geoff was born in Fortuna, California, and was raised in San Diego. His father manages country clubs and his mother is a nurse. He is the middle child of three boys. His parents divorced when he was young and although they live in different states—his mom remained in California and his dad moved to New Orleans—they stay in touch.

"Their relationship is complicated, but I appreciate that they can get along for the sake of our family," Geoff says.

As a child Geoff admits to being a problem. He was diagnosed with ADHD but refused to take his medication. He hid the pills in a secret drawer in his dresser. He got expelled from two different high schools, one for putting a cherry bomb in a toilet and the other for having a knife in school. He was placed with other "problem" teens at a continuation high school near his home.

"Me and my brothers, we were all hellions," says Geoff. "It was so hard for my mom to raise three boys." Despite that rough patch, Geoff values his family and is grateful for their continued love and support. His mom is from Ireland and "had to be tough to put up with me and my brothers."

"I'm so lucky," he says. "My mom is proud of me."

While at this continuation school, Geoff met a teacher who would turn his life around. "Ken Oleno was the first teacher that I really cared about," says Geoff. "He didn't care who I was or what I had done to get placed in this school, he just wanted me to graduate. Mr. Oleno set an example for how people should be treated. I was a troubled kid and a terrible student, but he showed me compassion. I treat people the way I do because of him."

After graduation, Geoff enrolled in culinary school. While he has worked for a time in the culinary and hospitality industry, the idea of spending his time indoors in a hot box kitchen wasn't for him. Geoff longed for the freedom of the open street.

He spent the next several years honing his juggling craft and perfecting his relationship-building skills on stages, underground, and at festivals. To keep things fresh, he was obsessive about improving his performance and incorporated many unusual items into his ever-changing act. Straightjackets, fire, bowling balls, knives...nothing was off limits.

Perhaps what he worked on the most, however, was his ability to connect with his audience—all different audiences.

"I was born with the gift of gab," Geoff says. "I got that from my dad." He describes his father as a conservative man who believed in his kids and supported them in their pursuits. When Geoff moved to New Orleans to be with his dad, he worked at a five-star resort on weekends and busked on the city streets most nights—all nights. That dichotomy was too much for Geoff. He convinced his dad to let him try making it full-time as a street performer. His dad, surprisingly, agreed and dropped him off downtown. Geoff is still grateful that his father believed in him enough to give him the freedom to make it on his own.

Life can be tough for buskers. Because their money is often out in the open, they are frequently targeted by snatchers and thieves. A piece of advice that Geoff learned early? "Never count your money on the pitch," he advised sternly. "Someone is always watching you." Geoff also admits that he carried a stun gun with him during his early days.

A few years ago, his mom and dad surprised him by flying to Wisconsin to see one of his shows at the Renaissance

Faire about forty minutes south of Milwaukee. The fact that his parents still talk despite the years and distance pleases Geoff. "I excel when I'm nervous and I was really nervous at that show for both of them to finally see what I do, together." He nailed his act. He even brought a little boy to tears for teaching him how to juggle, which was something he wanted to learn how to do. The crowd went crazy and his parents beamed with pride.

"They got to see for themselves that I'm not your average birthday clown," says Geoff. "I am driven to affect people; to make them happy."

This past year, Geoff got married to a beautiful woman he met at a different Renaissance Faire down South. She is a massage therapist who provides massage services to performers during the week and then performs herself on weekends. They are now building a home on twenty-five acres of land that her parents own in a one-stoplight town in Virginia.

While Geoff finally has roots, he has no plans to leave the road anytime soon. Last year, his first as a married man, he clocked in over 400 shows across the US, including a two-month residency in Milwaukee. He still busks on a pitch at festivals, but most of his appearances now are paid gigs on center stage, usually in front of an enthusiastic crowd of enthralled kids.

Even people who make a career out of change, change. Geoff always connected with kids and recognized his own ability to have a meaningful effect on them. It was a statement of the obvious by one of his colleagues that helped him intentionally steer his career in a different direction.

"You have that kid thing," chided a fellow entertainer after a family-friendly gig. "Kids love you and respond to you more than anyone else I've seen."

Those were the inspiring words Geoff needed to reinvent himself as an adult, not just his act. Geoff joined forces with the Milwaukee Public Theater, an organization that recognizes the empowering and healing benefits of the arts and is dedicated to making the arts accessible and available to all people, to discuss ways to use their gifts and resources to help more kids.

They applied for and received a grant to create a circus-themed curriculum that would help kids learn about the importance of good nutrition. Twice a week for four years, Geoff would go into public schools and used games and performance tools to help kids make healthy choices. They called him their teacher.

Also during that time, Geoff rented space in Milwaukee to pilot a circus school. He and his circus art friends offered daily classes in juggling, magic, aerial, hoops, Spanish web, and overall performing. Classes filled up, especially aerial silks and juggling. He was doing something he'd never thought a problem kid like him would do: own and operate a business.

No sooner had he started making plans to expand the program when the building changed hands and his school at that location had to close. From both of those professional experiences, Geoff learned a lot about business operations, negotiations, promotions, and talent management. He was surprised to discover that he had a passion for the business-end of entertainment and continues to provide the services he did as the owner of his school without the building.

"I'm basically the clown mafia," he says, with only a hint of sarcasm.

There are thirty-six local entertainers who are available to Geoff when businesses call. As a master relationship builder, Geoff has maintained connections with all of the event planners he has worked with over the years—including me. I've contacted Geoff several times since that first Summer Soulstice for entertainment purposes. And I'm not alone. His phone rings and his annual calendar gets booked. Which is a good thing, because the business of busking has changed significantly.

One big change is that people no longer carry walking-around money. It's more difficult to drop a few bucks into a guitar case when walking by. In response, a busker advocacy organization developed an app that would allow people to make tips and buy music from their phones, without exchanging cash.

Gypsy Geoff doesn't have this app. On behalf of his entertainers, Geoff advocates that his entertainers be paid living wages for the valued services they provide. When he's not handling their business, he's lifting them up with encouragement.

"There's a lot of doubt in this industry," he explains. "We're always wondering if our skills are good enough or if our act is funny enough. I say to them, 'Don't low ball yourself. If you do you will lower the value of all performers in town.'"

Geoff and I made a date to fish on the Milwaukee River. Inclement weather drove us indoors instead. We split a pizza and caught up on life and business. I asked him what would happen if his body ever wears out and he can't travel and perform anymore. He took a long sip of the pineapple cocktail he was drinking and said, "If I lost it all tomorrow, it would not bother me. I know how to fish and I know how to make enough for today. That has always been enough."

CHAPTER EIGHT

ANGEL IN THE MORNING

———

Again, Angel's dream is to start an urban fishing charter business so he can teach people to fish and show them his favorite spots in his beloved city—spots that people who have lived in Milwaukee their entire lives would never come across without his guidance.

"Urban Fishing with Angel" is the working title of his business; his daughter came up with it and he smiles shyly whenever he says it aloud. He has an idea of what the logo should look like and plans to ask a tattoo artist friend to design it. I offered to help him review designs because I wanted to make sure his brand isn't so edgy that it scares potential female customers away. I also reminded him that if he is going to include women, he needs to think about snacks. His idea is to include sandwiches with group outing packages and has already discussed menus with his favorite bar that is most famous for their Rueben. I suggest that he consider a multi-tier program, so he can offer a range of options from hot food to snacks and wine. I was sure to emphasize that wine would be a prime selling point.

He has to start slowly because his day job as a maintenance manager has him working odd hours. In the meantime,

Angel's on the look-out for a second job so he can treat his family to a trip to New Orleans in a couple months to attend a niece's wedding. The niece is actually his long-time girlfriend's niece, but to Angel, the loved ones of his loved ones are family.

I was apprehensive for our first outing. While I had a good feeling about Angel, we had only met once before and we were going to a place that I'd never been on a river that I hadn't yet fished. When I told Brett that I made plans to meet a stranger in a secret Milwaukee canal, he had questions. Not big questions, like "Who is this guy?" or "Have you thought this through?" or "Are you nuts?" Instead, he asked me questions about my preparedness to fish. Questions like, was my pole properly strung and did I know which lures did what? The truth is that I didn't even know how to put the back seat down in my car to fit my pole inside. I wasn't prepared and I didn't know which bits did what. Nonetheless, I packed up my car that first Saturday night in preparation for my morning date with Angel.

That morning my alarm didn't wake me up; severe thunderstorms did. Our power was out and our basement took in water overnight. It would take hours to clean. The forecast for the rest of the day was ominous, with tornado watches in surrounding counties. This was, in sum, an awful day to learn to fish. I checked my phone to see if Angel called or texted to suggest a different date. He hadn't. I got ready but assumed that we would reschedule once he checked the radar. He didn't cancel. I wanted Angel to think that I was tough and worthy of his time, so I didn't cancel. It felt like I was in a game: who would say "uncle" first?

I learned in our first meeting that *nothing* prevents Angel from fishing. When he can, he likes to fish early in the morning to make sure he gets it in each day. He has fishing friends everywhere but mostly fishes by himself so he can be spontaneous. He keeps two poles, a net, a tackle box, and boots in his car so he can stop off at a water spot between errands and on his way to and from work.

The rain that pounded my windshield on my way downtown that morning made it difficult to see. Cars were pulled over under overpasses to wait out the driving hazards. Again, I checked my phone. No message from Angel.

It stopped raining just as I hit the city. We were meeting at Angel's favorite fishing spot on the Menomonee River, near Milwaukee's train station and "Tent City," a homeless encampment located underneath a highway corridor. Tent City had been in the news all summer because the hundred or so occupants residing there had been ordered to vacate the public premises by the end of October. Now, that deadline was looming large. It's easy to miss the colorful tents, couches with mismatched cushions, and shopping carts filled with cardboard, plastic bags, newspapers, and other treasures, under the highway during the urban bustle of everyday life. On early Sunday mornings, however, when you're the only one on the road, it is impossible to ignore the signs of life, struggle, and community that the temporary residents construct. On my first drive by, I noticed a youngish African American man with dreads wearing dark sunglasses, jeans, and a multi-colored, hooded Mexican Baja jacket. He sat on a green couch, likely squishy from the storms, facing the road underneath the overpass. He puffed a cigar and blew perfect smoke rings that added to the black fibrous storm clouds parked above. I wondered how the treacherous thunder and lightning must boom and clap, echoing through their vantage point under the freeway. It must have felt like the highway would collapse from the rapturous hits that pummeled our city overnight. I dreaded that I would probably experience it for myself because the storm was set to re-strike soon.

Angel's car was parked a couple blocks away. When he saw me pull up, he hugged me hello like we were old friends. "Good morning Leeza, welcome to my favorite spot!" he said, proudly with his hands in a grand gesture. I don't think he noticed that it was starting to rain again. If he was nervous, he certainly didn't show it. When we finished our hug, he tapped my shoulder and began talking; he kept his eyes focused on mine when we spoke. He made me feel comfortable right off the bat, despite the fact that we were definitely starting to get wet. He was better looking than I remembered, though he wore the same bass hat with sunglasses over the bill. Instead of work pants, he had on cargo shorts and a tight fitted T-shirt that showed off his summer tan and muscles. He was freshly shaved for our Sunday morning in the rain, and I could detect a hint of a musk-scented aftershave.

I, on the other hand, was a frump. I didn't want the whole male-female thing to get in the way of our first fishing lesson, so I erred on the side of Wisconsin hick, with a hint of storm protection. My ensemble included dirty tennis shoes, baggy jeans, a black T-shirt with a stretched-out neck, and—to top it off—a Home Depot trucker hat. My intention with this ridiculous costume was to look like I fit in, but it actually made me stand out like the poser I was.

We arranged ourselves under a nearby viaduct just before another storm rolled in. The faux shelter did little to prevent the side soaking we endured from the thunder winds blowing off Lake Michigan. Six casts in and we were drenched. We kept right on casting. I remembered that I had two plastic garbage bag ponchos in my trunk from a family trip to Niagara Falls a year prior. They were crunched in the spare tire compartment of my trunk, which was just far enough away that I decided to wait out the rain to get them. When the rain slowed just a little, I broke into a run toward my car to fetch them.

We were strangers on a stormy Sunday morning in the City of Milwaukee, in matching blue plastic garbage bag ponchos. Our inaugural fishing outing was off to a shaky start. Nonetheless, Angel was determined to continue with my lesson. After a period of silence and a break in the clouds, Angel cleared his throat and spoke like he had planned his words carefully. "Leeza, there are three things that I want you to know about fishing. The first is to always carry a net," he said without looking at me. I couldn't help but notice that he did not have a net.

"And two, keep your tip up." He didn't have to explain the significance of this rule to me. When we walked over to our spot I had lazily carried my pole at my side and hooked my lure into the weeds. It was so wedged in there that he needed to help me sort it out.

"The final rule is to have fun," he said. "I believe in happiness. It's all about fun, Leeza. I firmly believe that the fish respond to how you're feeling. If you feel positive and are having fun, the fish will be drawn towards you. If you're negative, they stay away. Just like people."

Angel finds happiness in the simple things. "As longs as there's enough money left over for a twelve pack, I'm good," he added. This attitude got him through some pretty dark days, days when even the fish weren't biting.

Nearly twenty years ago, Angel was laid off from his maintenance job. Ever the optimist, he saw transition as an opportunity to start his own business. He left his handyman days behind and became a candy man instead. He and his friend rented a corner storefront in a west side neighborhood close to the bar they frequented. For nearly ten years, they worked long hours selling candy, Chicago dogs, and beef for very little pay. His once active, outdoor lifestyle was gone. Instead, he found himself stuck indoors and chained to an unsuccessful business venture, with no exit strategy. He grew depressed and ate and drank himself into a soul-crushing routine that left him overweight and empty. Eventually the pair lost their business, and Angel lost nearly everything he had. For nearly a year, he bounced between friends' couches and his car while he hustled side jobs to get back on his feet again. He washed dishes, cut lawns, removed snow, and cleaned buildings just to stay afloat. When things got really bad, he called his father in Puerto Rico and cried. With the support of his father and friends, Angel steadily crawled back up.

About two years ago he returned to his handyman roots and landed a job as a maintenance manager at a hotel chain. This job would lead to other opportunities within that hotel and on to others in the same company. Once he got back into a normal routine, Angel started taking care of his health again and lost thirty pounds. He likes his job and is pleased to have a regular schedule with plenty of time for fishing. He is also enjoying life with his girlfriend of nearly fifteen years, Kay. They share a nice home in the southwest side of Milwaukee and enjoy spending time with family. Together they have a bunch of kids and grandkids, and tons of nieces and nephews. What they don't do together, however, is fish. Kay doesn't like to fish. She likes to play Bingo at the casino near the canal where Angel fishes. They leave the house together and both do what they like to do on their days off.

We packed up our poles just as the sun started shining hotly down on the city. Our damp bodies finally dried, but our shoes still squished as we walked to our cars. We didn't have too much action that morning—Angel had caught one small bass towards the end of our time together. I commented that we need to be more positive next time to attract more fish and he replied, "I'm having the best year of my life, the fish will feel that and they will come. Just be patient, Leeza."

CHAPTER NINE

FINDING YOUR LIGHT

———

Dana doesn't fish. What draws her down to Milwaukee's rivers is even more elusive than a quest for the coveted sixteen-inch salmon in September. Behind their Canon EOS 5D, this self-trained photographer sharp shoots some of Wisconsin's rarest and most treasured birds in their utterly unfettered habitat. Her famously fickle subjects, preferably blue herons and hummingbirds, seem to be in on the photo shoot. They swoop, fly, feed, protect, and hunt on cue and they always seem to find their best light.

"I'm there so often they don't run away from me anymore," Dana quietly stated.

Everything Dana says is quiet and factual. She doesn't mince words. And she doesn't hide from her past.

While Dana wants to share her photographs with others, she is also uncomfortable that her work is getting recognized. When she started to frequent the parks back in 2018, it was the vastness and anonymity of Milwaukee's public green spaces that gave Dana a profound sense of peace and acceptance—desires Dana has craved her entire life.

Dana is actually hard not to recognize. The fifty-two-year-old father of two recently celebrated her fourth birthday as a woman. Her gender confirmation surgery was on August 11, 2015. Every year on that day, Dana posts about the experience on Facebook. As she affirms, "I didn't change my gender, I've always been female. This is the day I became who I've always been."

Dana stands squarely at five-feet and eleven-inches tall. Her shoulder-length hair is pulled back in a ponytail, with a nice curl to her bangs that softly frames her face. Dana has intense green eyes that are hiding behind dark sunglasses, a sharp nose, and is "lucky toothed"—*dents du bonheur* is the French term for the gap between the two front teeth. In most cultures, the chasm is normal and sometimes even sexy. In America, however, this condition is called "diastema," and there is a cosmetic procedure to correct it. As long, of course, as a person has the money to pay for it.

Dana doesn't have much money. Her divorce, bankruptcy, and injuries from a bike accident have forced her to move back home with her parents. Dana lives in the basement of her childhood home in a small suburb outside of Milwaukee. Right next door to this home is the home that Dana created when she was living as a man with a wife and two children a lifetime ago—when Dana was David.

"I spent a lifetime playing a character," Dana explained.

Dana remembers an incident that took place when she was just eight. Her conservative Christian parents hosted guests for dinner one evening and Dana was invited to join them at the table. The dinner discussion led to a righteous table-wide consensus that same-sex relationships were wrong. Even though Dana was living as David, Dana understood that they were condemning what was inside of her—what was waiting desperately to get out.

"It obviously wasn't the time to tell them that I was a girl inside," Dana conceded. "I kept my story to myself for a long time and only recently started to understand the consequences of that decision."

Dana's childhood memories are complicated because in every experience etched in her memory, Dana was David. "David" was the oldest of three children: two boys and a girl, in a religious family. Their dad was an accountant and CFO for a local company and their mom was a nurse. As a side hustle, the family started a baseball card and sports memorabilia business. Despite not having a sports enthusiast in the family, the business expanded to two stores at its peak. It was a family affair and afforded them opportunities to travel to various conventions across the country. They eventually sold the stores when none of the kids expressed an interest. Both parents are now comfortably retired.

Upon graduation from high school, "David" enrolled at the local university to study management information systems. While there, a neighbor of the family set "David" up on a blind date with a young woman. That woman would soon become "David's" wife. They were so excited to marry they didn't even wait for graduation. The young couple married in a traditional Lutheran ceremony and held their reception in a now-defunct supper club in their suburban neighborhood. In a circuitous turn of events, the newlyweds purchased their matchmaking neighbor's home and moved in right next door to where Dana was raised.

"As soon as we got married, I realized that I had a huge learning curve ahead of me," shared Dana. "I had to learn how to be a husband and manage the dysphoria and confusion that was brewing inside of me."

Together, the couple had two children, a boy and a girl. They maintained a traditional family life in which the father earned the money and the wife stayed home to raise their children.

"David" worked as an IT Manager at a regional architecture firm. As their family grew, "David" began to feel more and more dysphoria with the male body parts and the various gendered roles, including husband and father. The birth of their daughter was the turning point, Dana admits openly. Dana wanted to be the one to experience childbirth and be her mother but couldn't within the gender in which they were born. This dysphoria turned into depression. Severe depression.

"I became a workaholic because it was easier to be away from my family than to face what I knew was unavoidable." Dana could sense that everything was about to end.

With the help of a therapist "David" had been seeing to help with depression, "David" came out about feeling trapped in the wrong body—a male body. This brave announcement was the first falling domino a series of events that led the couple to move to separate bedrooms, and virtual separate corners of the world. In complete isolation, the two of them ruminated on their family's fate alone. They couldn't go back. They couldn't stop the inevitable. Each day brought more distance in the family. "David" was even barred from the dinner table and ate alone downstairs while the rest of the family sat together in the kitchen.

It was on Father's Day in 2014, that "David" was asked to move out of the house. "David" still had a computer science degree from a respected university and still had twenty-five years of experience working in architecture and design.

"David" was still a father. But still, "David" lost everything. Father's Day now, for Dana, is a very difficult day.

Most of the things and people in Dana's former life ran away as soon as Dana started to honor and live her truth, but her colleagues and bosses at the architecture firm stuck around...for a time. At first, Dana led two lives openly. On weekends she wore dresses and wigs out in public. She went to the mall, dances, out to dinner, and the parks in full makeup and heels—experimenting with looks and personas. During the week, it was all business for the person still presenting as a man, but slowly making the transition to her true self.

When Dana finally made the decision to confirm her real gender, she had to make big changes before the big change. Of all the baggage that Dana carried—guilt, sadness, anxiety, shame—her excess weight was the biggest obstacle to her ultimate goal. She needed to lose a hundred pounds before the surgeon would consider performing the procedure. Highly motivated, Dana made major lifestyle changes and achieved the required weight.

While she was living both lives, her weekend look began to creep into the office and colleagues began asking questions. Dana was relieved to finally share her real self with those with whom she'd worked for over two decades. Some of her coworkers took it in stride and others struggled.

"Everyone has different levels of tolerance," Dana said with a shrug.

Dana also struggled. She maintained her job throughout the transition and recovery but had much work yet to do on her look, especially in professional settings. In the beginning, Dana overdid her newfound femininity. She wore wigs, dresses, and jewelry to work. Perhaps her biggest faux-pas was inappropriate shoes on a job site—a mistake rookies make, not veterans of the industry.

"I learned to never wear heels to a job site," Dana now quips, without even a crack of a smile. Despite her missteps, Dana slowly got the hang of presenting as a woman. Perhaps the most difficult lesson was learning to dress down.

On the day we meet at the park, Dana dresses casually, her style of jeans and shorts is high-waisted and smartly mom-ish. No nonsense. A quest for the nonsensical, however, is what initially brought the two of us together. Dana and I had both tried our hand at improv comedy with Milwaukee's own ComedySportz a couple years prior.

ComedySportz is an improvisational comedy organization that started in Milwaukee in 1984. The format of a ComedySportz match features two teams of improvisational performers (players), competing in various improv games and scenes, with audience members judging results and awarding points. In every match, a referee monitors the action, awards points, and administers fouls as necessary.

Dana signed up for the evening workshops to practice living and speaking as a woman. She was fresh out of gender confirmation surgery and needed some polish and panache.

"The improv community is so supportive," she gushed. "They take anyone in."

As for me, I was suffering from a late onset case of the stage yips. As my professional career grew, I needed to get over stage freight and increase my public speaking competency.

We met on Monday nights. Me, Dana, and sixteen other people from all walks of life hoped to discover a talent for making people laugh. Our class of wannabes included: two mailmen, a recycling engineer, two artists, one musician, a barista, three people in sales, and an accountant.

For eight weeks our motley group practiced mime games, worked on our gibberish, and embraced the idea of offerings to prepare for our first show in front of family and friends. An "offering" in comedy is a gift that one comic sets up for another to seize upon for the big laugh. It takes time to get to know the comedic repertoire of others. It takes alcohol, too. Our Monday night crew ended class each night at an Irish bar down the street.

Neither Dana nor I were particularly funny. Dana made some progress toward her goal of presenting as a woman and I gained more confidence being in front of an audience. On a stage filled with funny people, we were the "straight men" in the group.

Dana's life took a drastic turn for the worse soon after we left the stage. I voyeured her series of events from the safe distance of my keyboard. It was too sad for trite comments of thoughts and prayers from a lame comedian like me, so I stayed mostly silent and kept my watchful distance.

Dana likes to bicycle and has ridden the Milwaukee trails since high school. She made a habit of posting her near-daily bike outings, and I paid attention to the posts and noted that she was showing more confidence with each new trail or distance conquered.

About six months after our comedy careers ended, Dana stretched her biking limits and took a new route along the hills and narrow high ways of Wisconsin's hilly farmland landscape. Rounding a sharp turn, she misjudged a grate in the road. From there, she remembers just two things before waking up in the hospital: the 38 Special song playing on her iPad and the cracking sound her bike made as it slid out from under her. Then things went black.

It was exactly one hour and fifteen minutes before Dana woke up. Dana knows that because her fitness device tracked her movements and time-stamped the exact moment that she lost consciousness. A stranger found her and called 911. This accident, this simple sports injury, spiraled her fragile life out of control. It wasn't losing her family or confirming her gender that caused Dana to lose everything. She had been hanging on by a thread up to this point. This accident cost Dana everything: her savings due to medical expenses and her independence. Because of her head injury, she could no longer live alone. Broke and broken, she moved into the basement of her parents' home, the one next to the house Dana once shared with a family, of which she was the father. There are new neighbors now. Her ex and their children moved away about a year after that one Father's Day.

Dana's headaches from the accident make her want to die. Her sensitivity to light and noise make it difficult to be out in public, especially in the heat and sun. The restorative parks in and around the city are her only solace. Dana has a suicide note that she keeps in an old dresser in the dark basement. Dana thinks that her death could serve a purpose.

"My note might help people understand what I'm going through," Dana said. "It could lead to greater acceptance."

On good days Dana brings her camera to the parks. Lately she goes to the parks most days.

"That's my time to be alone," Dana explained. "I don't worry about anyone bothering me." Dana and the birds do their private dance together in the sunlight for her lens to capture majestically. The birds see Dana for the quiet artist she is. I suggest that she consider doing more with her photography, so that more people could be exposed to her beautiful work. Dana shuts me down flatly. "It's about my journey, not the pictures."

The people who do follow Dana online, and the occasional person who recognizes her at the park, don't know her journey. They see this tall woman with wispy bangs and lucky teeth as simply an artist. Dana struggles with this. She feels disingenuous, like she's keeping a secret. Secrets have caused too much pain Dana's life.

"All I know is that I can't run from my past and I can't run from my problems; the baggage always accumulates."

* * *

A few months later, Dana and I met for lunch. She arrived first and waited for me on a bench in the lobby. Had Dana not been the only person there I would have looked right past her in search of my masculine, slightly awkward friend. Dressed in a black sweater with shoulder cut-outs and black pants, Dana stood up to greet me with a grace that was missing before. She wore dangling, dark sparkle earrings, a long black pearl beaded necklace, and had blonde highlights in her hair which was styled in a low ponytail with swooping bangs. Dana's lipstick was soft pink, her eye shadow subtle purple, and her eye-liner formed a striking up-tilt to her gaze. Dana looked pretty, confident, and content.

I'm a hugger, so we hugged. I made a note to myself, though, to ask Dana if it's okay to hug the next time we meet. She'd enjoyed much progress since our summer morning in the park. Some health wins, more attention for her photography, and a therapist who seems to be helping. The biggest change, however, is that she put herself out there in the dating world. Dana met several potential suitors and found a man who made her want to spruce herself up again. Dana doesn't know where this will go but is happy to feel some hope again.

"Maybe it's silly, but I still do want to get married and wear a dress," Dana affirmed.

Over gluten-free pizza and salad, we caught up on our friends from ComedySportz and swapped Milwaukee parks and rivers stories. Near the end of lunch, Dana brought a few of her photographs to share with me. One, was a group of men lined up along and in the Milwaukee River at the start of salmon season, and the other two were of a bald eagle that she captured at rest and in flight in the park where we'd met up. Dana matted the eagle shots to show her therapist that morning. She expected to use them to guide a discussion about personal freedom and how she was working to be free herself. As she drove to the appointment, however, the thought struck Dana that nothing is free. No living creature is free. The eagle, the very symbol of freedom, is governed by nature. The eagle must live where there is food, safety, and water. The bird Dana photographed would soon have to leave this habitat for open, unfrozen water. All the birds Dana dances with will be forced to move, adapt, or die from the wrath of a Wisconsin winter.

"I realized today that freedom is just an illusion," Dana concluded. "We're all confined to different things, different people, different challenges. We think we want freedom, but what we really want is the ability to adapt to what life brings."

Dana is still a work in progress, but her smile, gap and all, was wider than I had ever seen before. We ended our meal with another hug and that reminded me that I should have asked first. Next time, I'll remember.

CHAPTER TEN

CATCH AND RELEASE

At the dark end of every single cast could lurk the biggest catch of your life. That addictive tension between anticipation and the unknown keeps anglers coming back to the water for another day and another chance to conquer what they can't see but know is down there. Five outings in and I still hadn't earned my own fish story—I had yet to experience the irresistible effect that one simple, mysterious nibble could have on the rest of the day.

One of Angel's favorite fishing places was at the river between the Harley Davidson Museum and the Milwaukee Post Office. One Sunday, when we were there over Labor Day Weekend, the museum was hosting a party. Every Labor Day weekend Harley Davidson hosts a Milwaukee Rally that offers live entertainment and activities at multiple locations throughout town. Around forty thousand riders from all over the world take this yearly pilgrimage to Harley's homeland. Angel and I set ourselves up on the river in the center of the party, near the band.

We discovered that we both loved heavy music and we each knew all the words to the Heart, Iron Maiden, Guns & Roses, and AC/DC songs that serenaded us throughout the morning. We sang and cast and compared notes about local bands, favorite concerts, and personal soundtracks.

Our mere presence attracted several revelers to wander from the party to the river to see what we were catching. We made a curious pair: I was in full makeup that day and my usual clothes because I had plans to get together with friends for brunch; Angel went full camouflage. To the museum staff, we were regulars. They liked to sneak smokes in by us on weekends during their breaks. They all had fish stories to swap. Angel would pull out his phone with the cracked screen to share his photos of the week. They were all interested in his trophy catches.

When we weren't visited, we sat on the rocks with our poles in the water, bobbed our heads to the music, and chatted about Puerto Rican food and our mutual love of tamales from a local Mexican grocery shop. He shared a recipe for yellow rice that involves spices that I hadn't heard of before. He freezes cubes of broth with his proprietary blend of Puerto Rican spices so he can have his native rice on a weeknight basis. He was going into detail about this technique when his pole visibly bounced. We were both startled. For the first time, he handed his stick to me.

I'm ashamed to say that I got scared.

Before I started this adventure, I psyched myself into the possibility that I would have to touch a dead fish. My neighbor fished when I was a kid. A bunch of us watched for him to pull his boat up his driveway on late Saturday afternoons in hopes that he'd caught fish. When he did, we got to watch him clean them. Sometimes he would even let us touch them first. He made his counter out of a two-by-four and a pair of saw horses that he set up in the back end of his yard, to avoid getting guts too close to his home. He pointed out the anatomy of fish when he made cuts. When he was done, he put the fish in an outdoor smoker he made out of a wooden box, tin foil, and a fire pit with scented wood chips. Smoked fish is one of the smells of my childhood.

The fish my neighbor brought home were dead. The fish he sometimes let me touch were dead. He caught them, pulled the hook out of their squirming mouths, and then somewhere between his boat and our awaiting eyes, the fish were no longer alive. I never stopped to think about the mysterious chain of events in between.

When I pulled up Angel's small-mouth bass, I faced a living, flapping fish for the first time and it was squirming for its life. I screamed, "Angel, help me!" Then I went even further by shouting, "Don't make me do this, I'm afraid!"

I managed to reel the fish in but couldn't bring myself to grab and steady it enough to pull the hook out. My heart was pounding and I felt an intense fear that was entirely unexpected and completely embarrassing. Angel graciously pulled the hook out, but he wouldn't let me get away without a picture. Despite my protests, he handed me the three-pound scaly wiggle fish with important instructions: "Avoid the fin, Leeza. It could cut you!"

What? I was gearing myself up for the feel of the scales and the tiny teeth blades but wasn't warned about a sharp fin. This was news that required processing. I was afraid all over again. He handed me the fish anyway, and commanded that I stick my thumb firmly in the fish's mouth to hold it still for a photo. I managed to assume the church offering pose just long enough for him to snap a shot. When he was done, I carefully released it back into the water and felt unwarranted pride in myself and my accomplishment. Perhaps because

Angel was so excited for me. "You did it Leeza! You caught a fish!"

* * *

I was in the presence of greatness the day I saw "the kid" catch twenty-nine fish in just over an hour at the falls of the Milwaukee River. The young angler perched his small body on a log that was wedged between rocks at the top that created a shaky plank only a person of his size and dexterity could utilize. There were undoubtedly more fish caught that day. I only started fence-posting when his multiple catches caught my attention. "The kid" was a young teenager and wore a wrestling shirt from an area junior high school. He was in the zone and didn't seem to notice that the people around him had put down their poles to watch this perfect dance between boy and nature.

There was a different vibe to the riverbank that day. In addition to some of the usual fellas, there was a mom and three very young kids who recklessly broke fishing protocol by drilling their hooks into the water too close to other lines. If any one of them had gotten a nibble, lines would have undoubtedly become tangled. Each of the kids had the same peculiar cast: a speedy sidearm with a firm bat down at the end. They kept their elbows tucked into their sides and relied on their wrists more than the average angler. I smiled to myself when I realized that I'd been hanging around fishermen long enough to recognize a peculiar cast. I'd come a long way. The kids obviously did not learn this form from their mother. Hers was a gorgeous cast with a precision I hadn't seen from other anglers before. She marked a point in the river and hit her target cast after cast. Despite her grace, she did not make a catch.

"Did you hear about the forty-three-inch muskie?" shouted a man as he walked towards me on my usual perch. I had seen the man around before. He was a distinguished gentlemen in his mid-seventies who wore a brown leather bomber jacket, no matter the temperature. He didn't fish but he enjoyed his daily cigar along the bank. I wondered where he smoked his cigar during the winter months.

Before I had a chance to respond to his muskie question, he spread his arms apart the length of a good sized human to demonstrate what forty-three inches would look like if I added ten extra inches. It was apparently caught the prior week by an unrecognized angler just below the falls.

It had rained hard the night before and the grass and my picnic table were still wet. I sat on a plastic grocery bag that was loose in my trunk. My new stogie friend plopped down next to me on the wet wood before I had the chance to warn him. If he noticed the dampness on his bottom, he didn't care. I hadn't heard that specific story, but big muskie stories are a part of growing up in Wisconsin.

* * *

My "big muskie" story of the summer was actually a carp. Angel and I met earlier than usual on a Sunday morning in September because he had tickets to an afternoon Brewers game. We were the only signs of life in our corner of downtown Milwaukee, and neither one of us had yet to fully wake up. As always, we greeted each other with a hug and caught each other up on the events of our week. We talked so much over the summer that our family members were familiar to each other, even though they have yet to meet.

He liked to listen to music when he fished and alternated between salsa and New Orleans' jazz. That morning we grooved to The Neville Brothers, Dr. John, and Louis Armstrong's version of "When the Saints go Marching in." When that song came on, we both danced around like we were in a parade on Bourbon Street. I played the trombone in grade school and air-slid my instrument by the river up and down like a first-liner native. Angel was excited because he and his family would be in New Orleans on Saint Patrick's Day and their first order of business was to throw potatoes and cabbage at people from a float, which is apparently a thing in New Orleans. I had never heard of it, but I'd never been to New Orleans.

When our tiny parade ended, we got down to fishing. Angel strung his favorite chartreuse lindy jig to start with, absentmindedly tossed it in, and told me about a nighttime cleaning job he picked up to earn extra money. After that, our conversation inevitably turned to food. He had just watched a video about how to make the perfect potato pancake and was eager to make them for his family that evening. His recipe had sour cream in it which we both questioned for its ability to hold up on a heated skillet. He was looking at me at the time that he got a hard tug. His whole body heaved forward. The fish was deep and plunging deeper in the dark water— likely a bottom feeder. Angel went into battle and held his pole up as high as he could to keep the fish's mouth pointing up for control and keep the hook safely in place. Once the fish couldn't go downward it panic-swam back and forth and in circles until it eventually tired itself out. The fish forcefully led Angel about twenty feet down the riverbank. The scene reminded me of when I take my ninety-pound Labrador on a walk and get the usual "Who's walking who?" cracks from my neighbors. I set my pole down and followed him.

Finally, the fish tired out enough to be caught. I ran to get the net, which Angel then tucked under his arm. We could finally see just how big this catch was when it thrashed at the surface. "Look at that motherfucker, Leeza" shouted Angel. "It's a carp!"

The carp did not make it easy. Angel cranked it close enough to scoop with a net, but the crafty carp kept evading the web. Angel was on his knees now and fully extended over the water. With one hand he managed his writhing pole, and with the other, he scooped and missed. Scooped and missed. Obviously, his net was too small. I wondered if it could contain the fish even if Angel managed to get it in. I just stood there and watched.

It was a struggle that continued on land, once the fish did get itself caught in the net. Both of us were breathing heavy. This was the exhilarating moment that Brett compared to racing. The fish flopped its way in and out of Angel's arms as he tried to take the hook out. Its tail slapped Angel in the face and knocked his hat sideways. I don't know how, but he managed to get the hook out cleanly despite the tussle.

Once that happened the fish went stiff. Angel laid it on the dirt ground under the tree nearby. If it wasn't for its large, pulsating gills, I would have sworn that all the excitement killed it. "You watch him, Leeza. I gotta get the tape measure!" Before I could offer to go in his place, he was gone. I stared at the fish and it side-eyed me back without moving. The pulsing of its gill reminded me of the Apple computer light that breathes to let you know it's still on. I kept my distance because I was sure it was just playing possum before it jumped up with its sharp teeth and fin of blades to cut and slime me. My heart pounded. Again, I felt fear.

For Angel, fishing might actually be for the fish. Thoreau's quote about people who fish for reasons other than fishing doesn't entirely hold true with Angel. He never gets tired of catching fish and returns to the river every single day to get his fix.

Angel got back measured the length from tip to tail at thirty-two inches and the girth at the widest part at twenty-two. Then he mumbled off a formula that calculates the weight of the fish with those two data points. After rattling around some numbers in his head, he proudly announced that this fish was just over nineteen pounds. I silently questioned his math at the time but had no way to double check. When I got home I researched how to calculate the weight of fish and he turned out to be perfectly accurate.

He held up the fish to pose for his picture. I recognized the significance of this picture and had him do two poses in two different locations to make sure we had the right light and a bright smile on his good side. He would share these photos of this big catch through his cracked screen with all the visitors who would come to see us by the river in the city of Milwaukee.

CHAPTER ELEVEN

CHEERS

Fish get airborne in early fall. "Just wait til' salmon season, and they'll jump right in your net," was the sage comeback that seemingly every wise fisherman said to me when I disparaged the fact that I had yet to catch my own fish without assistance. Since I started fishing in spring, I had been waiting eagerly for salmon season.

Angel and I kicked off my virgin salmon season with whiskey shots early on a sunny Sunday in October. We had a lot to celebrate that morning beyond the anticipation of jumping fish. It was the first sunny day in over a week, Angel had just been offered a second job, which would help him get on top of bills and save for a family trip, and he was sporting a new net that he couldn't wait to show off.

It was a net rescue. Angel found it along the side of the riverbank near Miller Park, the home of the Milwaukee Brewers. He was there between rainstorms one morning because his usual spots were flooded out. The net is big-fish large and has a scoop that could hold a small child. Angel spent the week pulling debris out of the web so it would look nice for our debut.

I brought the whiskey. While Angel is normally a Miller High Life guy, Irish Whiskey is his official mark of a monumental occasion. To me, the start of salmon season was just such an occasion. I picked up a bottle of Tullamore Irish Whiskey, his favorite, the night before and tucked the bottle neatly in my new tackle box as a surprise. Angel brought his speakers and was playing salsa music that bounced happily off of the still morning water.

We met at our usual place in the canals facing the skyline just as the sun cast the first glow over the refurbished warehouses that stood taller in sun salutation. We walked out of the shadows to get as much warmth as we could on that crisp autumn start. Eager to get our hooks in the water, we both cast before we even got ourselves settled. By settled I mean before I had the opportunity to scroll through his week of fish photos through the cracked screen—our usual first order of business.

I pulled out the bottle midway through photo admiration and when he saw it, Angel exclaimed, "I love Wisconsin! What other state drinks this early in the morning?"

He opened the bottle and poured generously, three fingers full, in the clear plastic cups that I packed. "Wait Leeza!" he said when I started to take a sip. "Buen Provecho," he said, and held up his cup. He exclaimed it is a kind of cheers that his family says, and it roughly translates to "Whatever you got, enjoy it."

We sipped our whiskey, listened to the salsa music, and let our insides get as warm and dry as our faces felt in that morning sun. It was beautiful on the river. We both sat down on the rocks and lazily held our poles towards the water, making little effort to be tantalizing to the swimmers below.

We had no nibbles and nothing went airborne, but it was another great day at the water.

Neither of us could stay long. Angel and his girlfriend were hosting a birthday party that afternoon and he had a bunch of errands yet to run for the gumbo they were preparing. I had to get back to take Simon to a college fair. He had shortened his list of potential schools to seven and we were hoping to meet with a few of them that afternoon before the Packers kicked off later in the day.

Angel and I each had a few small sips left. He held up his shallow cup one more time and said to me, "To our kids' future." I couldn't think of a better toast than that. We clinked our cups and packed up to go our separate ways. Maybe it was a bit premature to cheers in the salmon; perhaps I jumped the gun. Regardless, I took him up on his toast to enjoy what I have.

What I had on that beautiful day in October was a son at home waiting for me to go with him to visit colleges. My time with him won't last forever, but what I have will always be my greatest joy. Cheers.

CHAPTER TWELVE

WITHOUT A NET

"Wake up, we're going to catch a whopper!" announced Brett as he barged into Simon's bedroom one late Saturday morning in fall.

Simon wasn't happy about the sleep interruption. He played football for his high school team and this was a rest and recovery day after a hard week of practice. Despite protesting, he got out of bed because he had promised to go fishing with Brett and me that day. We already purchased the one-day, non-transferable fishing licenses through the Wisconsin DNR's website for eight dollars each.

While they got ready, I went to the store to get an assortment of fishing snacks. There's a right snack for every occasion—a hospitality tip that is a trademark of my family's lineage. When we get together, we bring snacks. A base spread usually involves fruit like grapes or cherries, hand-held cheese like squeaky curds or string, chips, some sort of dip, and beer. If we don't coordinate snacks when my sisters and parents and I get together, we each bring a spread that, when combined, could rival a Superbowl party. This has become a big joke among the men who married into our munching family.

That morning I purchased a selection of bottled teas, organic beef jerky, various protein bars, and gummy worms to stuff in the snack pockets of my birthday tackle box.

We chose an urban park with a gorgeous river trail, a skate park, a popular beer garden, and live polka music on weekend afternoons. At noon when we arrived, the beer was already flowing and people were dancing with their heavy German steins to music performed by old men wearing lederhosen.

We carried our fishing poles with our tips up through the crowds to the Frankie Yankovic tune, "In Heaven There Is No Beer." Every Wisconsin resident knows the words to that song and has at one time in their lives kicked off their shoes to polka dance with grandma at a wedding.

Polka music and grandmas are quite prevalent at "Holy Land" weddings where I grew up and learned my greatest moves.

The "Holy Land" is the affectionate local name for all the farm towns in our area in Southeastern Wisconsin. Each one of them had a supper club, one gas station, three bars, and a church that they were named after. I have relatives from Saint Peter, Saint Charles, Saint Cloud, and Johnsburg (after Saint John). When there was a wedding out in the "Holy Land," everyone came ready to party after cleaning up from their evening milking.

The DJs in the Holy Land elegantly intersperse Polkas with wedding greatest hits, so there's something for everyone. For our family, the greatest hit is "Paradise by the Dashboard Lights" by Meatloaf. When that song comes on it's well known to clear the dance floor if you don't want to get flailed, swatted, shouted at, or humptied. That song has been "ours" since the day my dad installed a portable tape deck to the bottom of our kitchen cabinet. "Bat Out of Hell" was the only cassette we ever played in the deck, and we did so nearly every night during meal prep. We were versatile fans. If my dad was around he would take the male parts, but each of us could pitch in to complete the vocal cast. No matter who sang what, we all stopped what we were doing and shouted—to our neighbors' ire—the "Stop right there!" line. That was all of ours. The tape deck broke decades ago, but I imagine if we opened it up that lone tape would still be loaded and ready for family dinner.

The three of us took over a semi-private area just off the river path but in singing distance to our live polka back line. Once we got settled, Simon went straight for the beef jerky in the tackle box. Brett, wasting no time, made the first cast. As per usual with him, despite the fact that he hadn't fished since he was a kid, it was perfect. A straight cast with a good arc about twenty feet into the center of the rolling river. He cranked it in right away and did it again. Over and over and over.

It occurred to me when we got settled that we violated Angel's first rule of fishing: we didn't have a net.

When Simon was done with the first round of snacks, he threw rocks in the water. At first, he aimed for a tree across the river. Then, when he got bored with that, he took aim for Brett's hook wherever it was in the water. This did nothing to attract fish. When Simon was done with that, he went back for the rest of the snacks. I stuck my first cast in the mud below, which surprised all of us because the river seemed too high to make rock and mud hazards conceivable. It wasn't the best reflection of all that I had worked on throughout the summer.

Brett and I traded a few more casts. The polka band played another round of Yankovic's heaven and beer song. We were out of snacks and Brett and I were hungry for lunch. I was disappointed that we weren't having more fun. I arranged this day with a high expectation that the three of us would bond in this beautiful setting and naturally assume the classical archetype of a strong American family idling an afternoon together down by the river. I imagined that I would show off my new fishing skills, and that Brett and Simon would be impressed with my technique—perhaps be inspired to work on their own fishing game. After all, by then I could recognize the difference between a small and large mouth bass, I knew how to keep the pole up, I could speak passably about jigging and its benefits, and I developed a value for patience. Not bad for a rookie fisherman who hooked her own pants upon first cast. They were neither impressed nor inspired. They were bored and ready to go.

Before we left, I talked Simon into making three obligatory casts. He made them quickly with limp wrists and none of his usual athletic effort. I don't even think he looked in the river's direction. "There Mom, I fished with you," he said.

It was the fall of Simon's senior year in high school and it felt like we were in the biggest "last phase" of our lives. Simon's last first day. His last Homecoming. Last football game. Last, last, last. We were running out of time. We never bothered to teach him to fish. There were a lot of things we didn't teach Simon how to do. We didn't teach him to fill a water softener, or how to fix a toilet, or when to change a light fixture. We never took him to Europe or to see the Grand Canyon. He hadn't yet planted a garden.

There's something about waiting for fish to bite that sheds people of the armor they carefully construct around themselves. Strangers talk quietly about intimate things while they wait. People work through complicated issues in their lives while they wait. And anxious moms can seek the advice from fathers and mothers who have been there before while they wait.

In all the discussions I'd had with people from all walks of life, our river conversations inevitably led to parenthood.

Dana, who is navigating what it means to be a father as a woman and is working to fully accept herself. Keith, the son of Milwaukee's father of urban fishing and how he hopes to hold out his father's legacy. Geoff whose own father trusted him so much he allowed him to live on the streets to find himself as a performer and as a man. And Angel, the father of two, the grandfather of five, and the son of a Puerto Rican patriarch who raised Angel to be athletic, hardworking, and kind in the shadows of Wrigley Field.

We finally called it a day and packed up our stuff and walked toward the bridge leading up to the beer garden above. Simon tripped slightly on a branch and Brett said what he always says when someone trips, "Hey, who put that there?" Which prompted Simon to say, "I knew you were going to say that."

"Am I that predictable?" asked Brett knowingly.

"Yes, dad," replied Simon. "There are some things you always say, like when you yawn you always say 'yawn' and when you burp you always follow that up by saying 'burp.'"

I think all dads have their sayings. Like my dad, who starts every story with "It's really kinda funny" whether it's funny or not. My dad has so many annoying sayings that we can devote whole dinner conversations to quoting him. For example, he doesn't excuse himself quietly when he needs to use the restroom. Instead, he announces to the room that he has to go "tap a kidney" or "water some petunias." Whenever he meets someone new he introduces himself as "Mark Cody like Buffalo Bill." We are not related to Buffalo Bill Cody. And just about anything in life can be related back to his fraternity days or his time in the Army. These lines and their predictability are the shorthand that defines us as a family. Simon doesn't know it yet, but our insider language and corny jokes define him, too.

None of us felt like joining the polka party, so we decided to grab some burgers and custard at a favorite Milwaukee stop on the way home.

All three of us ordered cheeseburgers; Brett and Simon added chocolate malts. The place was packed and our order took a while. We waited in silence. Simon and Brett both scrolled on their phones. When our food was finally ready, we found a place to sit outside. Simon was still on his phone as I divvied up the food. I felt defeated that this time wasn't more meaningful. As we were in the year of lasts, everything felt like it was supposed to have meaning.

Between bites, Simon reacted to something that appeared on his screen. He turned to Brett and read aloud a story about a university football team and how they lost a game in overtime based on a bad kick. That led them to discuss college football scores coming in that day, which led them to discuss their fantasy football teams and the trades they made going into the weekend. After that they switched over to baseball to make World Series predictions. They compared calendars and bought tickets to one more Brewer game before the season would end.

That's when it hit me. Their love language is sports.

Simon wasn't terribly interested in learning how to fish. He is, however, interested in talking about football and baseball and basketball with Brett. I had been worried about the two of them. They might not have bonded the way I had scripted it in my head, but they did so, entirely on their own. And wherever Simon ends up, they will always have sports to bring them back together.

I stopped to consider why I started going fishing; perhaps I was hoping that through my experiences the two of them might be inspired to join me. And, from that first outing together as a family, we would have that one, lifelong thing that would become *our* thing. Some families have a band, some have a team, some have rituals and traditions. We, I thought, would have urban fishing.

On our way home the song "Blackbird" by the Beatles came on the radio. That beautiful song was the encore performance of the acoustic show that happened on North Avenue every Monday night when Brett and I crawled the bars twenty-five years ago.

Back then, we loved Monday nights. No cover, quarter taps, and two of the best musicians in the city breaking down to just them and their guitars. One of them channeled Bruce Springsteen and performed acoustic versions of "Growing Up," "Thunder Road," and "Saint in the City" like they were our songs, our anthems, in our city.

The other was an energetic, middle-aged Rastafarian. During the week, he swung his long graying dreads around recklessly while jamming to Bob Marley and island reggae, but on Monday nights, it was just him, his guitar, and a chair for his bad back. As a solo artist, he covered the Beatles, Blind Faith, and Mad Dogs and Englishmen. His version of "Blackbird" broke your heart. When he sang "Blackbird" on Mondays at midnight, you grabbed the hand of the person sitting next to you. You didn't sing along, you didn't take a drink of your cheap beer in a plastic red cup, you didn't look away.

The line, "You were only waiting for this moment to arise," was all of us in the bar, waiting for our moment. That song has a way of finding me at the stage in life when I need it most. This time, I was on the other end, preparing for my little bird to take flight.

Henry David Thoreau's words, "Many men go fishing all of their lives without knowing that it is not fish they are after," propelled me to learn to fish in Milwaukee's urban waters. I always knew it wasn't fish I was after. What I thought I would find through my journey along the riverbanks was the start of a meaningful, lasting way for Brett, Simon, and me to bond as a family. I imagined that my fishing would get *them* into fishing and that the three of us would always find our way back to each other along the banks of any water, wherever Simon's road leads. Just three poles, a couple of lindy jigs, good snacks, and a little water, and we would be "us" forever.

What I was after and what I found turned out to be different. Brett, Simon, and I are "us." We've had hard days and blocks of time where the elusive future wasn't inevitable. But we've also had a million little moments that solidify us as a family. Our unique bond will change and be challenged, but that's how it is supposed to be. No matter where Simon goes to school and what he'll study, there will always be football, basketball, and baseball that will keep us together.

My circuitous quest led me back to what it is I'm after. While it was never fish, I must admit that it has actually become fish. For it is salmon season after all, and I want Angel to take my picture with a big one.

APPENDIX

—

BOOKS

Thoreau, Henry David. 1908. *Walden, or, Life in the woods.* London: J.M. Dent.

Coelho, Paulo. 1998. *The alchemist.* [San Francisco]: HarperSanFrancisco.

Salinger, J. D. *The Catcher In The Rye.* Boston : Little, Brown And Company, 1991, c1946.

MOVIES

Foul Play Movie Directed by Colin Higgins. Paramount Pictures 1978

Say Anything Movie Directed by Cameron Crowe 20th Century Fox 1989

SONGS

"Cecilia" Simon & Garfunkel, 1970

"Into the Mystic" Van Morrison, 1970

"Grease" The original motion picture soundtrack for the 1978 film

"Endless Summer" Album Beach Boys, 1974

"The Twist" Chubby Checker, 1960

"Jack Straw" Grateful Dead, 1972

"Truckin'" Grateful Dead, 1970

"Yakety Sax" composed by James Q. "Spider" Rich and Boots Randolph, 1963

"When the Saints go Marching In" Louis Armstrong, 1938

"Paradise by the Dashboard Lights" Meat Loaf, 1977

"In Heaven There is no Beer" Frankie Yankovic version

"Blackbird" The Beatles, 1968

"Growing Up" (1973), "Saint in the City" (1973), "Thunder Road" (1975) Bruce Springsteen

MUSICIANS/BANDS MENTIONED

Nirvana

Pearl Jam

Heart

Iron Maiden

Guns & Roses

AC/DC

38 Special

Johnny Cash

The Neville Brothers

Dr. John (Malcolm John Rebennack Jr.,)

Bob Marley

Blind Faith

Mad Dogs & Englishmen

ACKNOWLEDGEMENTS

As a grateful and dutiful member of a mighty family pack, I have never walked alone. From my parents, sisters, grandparents, aunts, uncles, cousins, in-laws, and like-family friends, I've learned to persevere always, laugh inappropriately, love unconditionally, and recognize the blessings in each day. This book is my contribution to the storied family legacy.

I'm fortunate to have many friends who value loyalty, support, and forgiveness like I do. Many of the people in my life have been with me for twenty-five years or more and keep me grounded and healthy whenever I lose my way. I am who I am because of their collective imprints. They will each recognize something unique to them within the pages of this book.

My new friends made this book possible. Keith Garner, Geoff Marsh, Dana Kornitz, and Angel Perez saved a spot for me along the river and taught me how to embrace the unknown as I enter a new phase in my life.

Finally, this book is a love letter to my husband Brett and our son Simon.

Thank you to the following people who believed in me and supported this project early.

CAST SUPPORTERS

Albert, Lynn
Ansems, Tracy
Baker Mathu, Karen
Blaha, Julie
Brown, Kevin
Brylow, Darla
Burke Schumaker, Meghan
Burton, Katie
Cody, Mark and Mary
Cody, Paula
Cortinovis, Tim
Diederichs, Laurie
Doerfler, Daniel J
Dorff, Mindy
Flanagan, Nicole
Flierl, Jennifer
Gale, Mark
Gale, Mark
Gallun, Cynthia
Gerner, Steve
Gettelfinger, Lee
Halper, Christopher
Hoffman, Michele
Jackson, David
Jameson, Gretchen
Kauffman, Krista
Kitchen, Mike and Diane
Kittleson, David
Koester, Eric
Kornitz, Danielle
Kratcha, Lynn

Kraus, Sheri
Kriege, Kate
Lang, Jayne
Leighton, Ann
Liljegren, Brett
Liljegren, Peggy
Liljegren, Simon
Liljegren, Stephen
and Donna
Liljegren, Wade
Litman, Mike
Loucks, Molly
Lucchesi Taylor, Gale
Luettgen, Julie
Mauthe, William
McEuen, Jennifer
Melan, Cathy
Michel, Andrea
Montgomery, Todd
Nevicosi Staner, Angela
Paulsen, Martin
Pfeifer, Eileen
Randolph, Julie
Re, John
Rentscher, Mary E.
Resch, Tony
Richmond, Matthew R.
Sanchez, Jill
Siegle, Suzy
Smith, Laurie
Sproul, Linda

Stasiak, Bret
Sullivan, Ireene
Sullivan, Tim
Swangstu, Kristin
Thiel, Kali
Tuffey, Tracy

Turgeson, Kay
Waller, Debra
Weber, Anne
Westreich, Jane
Wilke, Jane
Zimmer-Anderson, Kathleen

Made in USA - Kendallville, IN
1085979_9781641375290
04.22.2020 1038